# This Book Is Dedicated and Belongs to:

_____

*whose address is:*

_____

_____

*Telephone:* ( ___ ) _____

*The*
# Self-Sufficient Woman

**(Things EVERY woman needs to know!)**

**by**
**LARRY PERRY, J.D.**

*Performance Press, Oak Ridge, Tennessee*

# *The* Self-Sufficient Woman

## *"Knowledge IS Power"*

Published by
Performance Press
Box 3194
Oak Ridge, TN 37831
(615) 483-8474

ISBN 0-942-44200-8

# Welcome to
# *The* Self-Sufficient Woman

The secret of making it as a single woman is peace of mind. Peace of mind comes from Power. **POWER COMES FROM KNOWLEDGE.** That is what this book is all about--gaining/collecting knowledge and information that will give you personal power. This workbook and its checklists/forms are designed to help you through the many details of suddenly becoming single. The book is to be used along with our course of the same name.

Most everyone respects books too much to mark them up with personal comments--that is why I chose to make this a combination reading and writing book...so that we can relax and have the best of both worlds.

Remember that the better organized you become, the easier it will be to deal with any situation. The hardest part is getting started. Don't expect to complete all the worksheets in one short period of time. Complete the ones you know the answers to NOW and begin to collect information on the others immediately. Try to have all the information completed within 30 days and you will feel better and more secure. Look for ideas that will help you in your daily life from the material contained here.

Once you complete the information required, fill in the Commitment Card in the back of this workbook and drop in the mail to me. By return mail you will receive a handy gift as a token of my appreciation. Keep this workbook handy so you will know where it is when you need to refer to important personal information if there is a crisis in your life.

*"You Cannot Consistently Perform in a Manner that is Inconsistent with the Way You See Yourself."*

# TABLE OF CONTENTS

*(The italic listing under each main topic is the list of checklists and charts for you to complete.)*

# How To Use This Workbook

This workbook is designed for YOU to help YOU. It requires your commitment to improve yourself. It is tested time and again with women just like you. IT WORKS!

First, thumb through the entire book just to get a feel of the material contained within these covers. Stop and glance at the pages that interest you and then continue on through the book.

Second, begin back at page 1 and take the Two Minute Quiz. Check your answers with those on the second page of the Quiz. All of these questions are discussed somewhere in this book.

The book covers many subjects in brief form. This is so that you can learn the basics and then continue to study those weak areas more in detail from other sources later. I want to acquaint you with many topics that may be foreign to you. The purpose is to give you knowledge in order to gain self-confidence in yourself and thus become self-sufficient. Remember, **Knowledge is Power!**

Look for ideas in the book that will help YOU. Read it several times and find new ideas each time that you overlooked on earlier readings. You will be surprised at how fast you learn.

When you finish, copy the poem entitled: "WINNERS" in your own handwriting and read it every day for 30 days when you first get up in the morning and when you go to bed in the evening. Thirty days...now that is not too much to ask...is it?

You are a WINNER! Otherwise, you wouldn't have bought this workbook to help you. Winners are readers.

Have fun and keep this book in a safe place with your other valuable papers. It will save you hours of work in emotional times.

*"A Winner Never Quits and*

*A Quitter Never Wins."*

# TWO MINUTE CHECK-UP

*(Take a few minutes and answer the questions below. Then check yourself with the correct answers on the next page. This will give you a good indication as to how carefully you need to read this wookbook and complete the information requested.)*

1. It is best to pay for everything with cash and never run up bills or borrow money if you can.
   ( ) True   ( ) False

2. If a person takes out a life insurance policy for $100,000 and pays the premiums, upon their death the full $100,000 is received by his beneficiary with no strings attached.
   ( ) True   ( ) False

3. A person should keep a will in a safe place, preferably a safety deposit box.

   ( ) True   ( ) False

4. If a husband dies, his wife may continue using their joint credit cards after notifying the card companies of his demise.

   ( ) True   ( ) False

5. If a woman with established credit needs to borrow money, she should do so only at her bank.

   ( ) True   ( ) False

6. The three kinds of car insurance that every woman needs are _____, _____, and _____.

7. The two items that every woman needs with her husband are a will and a _____.

8. The difference between a CREDIT card and a DEBIT card is _____.

9. In planning a budget a woman should allow about _____% of her income or the family income for housing.

10. There is a 30 day cooling off period for door-to-door sales contracts.
    ( ) True   ( ) False

11. A valid check may not be dated on Sunday or a Federal holiday.
    ( ) True   ( ) False

12. Mail order firms generally must fill orders within 30 days or offer your money back.   ( ) True   ( ) False

3

# Answers to Check-up Quiz

*(Below are the answers to the questions on the previous page that affect YOU!)*

1.  FALSE. You have no credit until you have borrowed some money and repaid it. Most everyone will encounter a time in their lives when they need credit. Paying for everything in cash does not create a credit record.

2.  FALSE. The $100,000 does not go to the beneficiaries if the person has taken out the policy and paid the premiums. It becomes a part of the estate and is subject to taxes which may run very high if the estate is large.

3.  FALSE. A safety deposit box is the WRONG place to keep a will. The box is usually sealed at the time of one's death. By the time it's opened, it may be too late to carry out some of the provisions of the will.

4.  FALSE. If a husband dies, a credit card company closes his account when they learn of the death. A wife is not allowed to continue using the credit cards even though their account was a joint one. She may reapply under her own name and will have to satisfy credit requirements.

5.  FALSE. A bank may charge more interest than some other lenders so it is not necessarily the best lender. The fact that a woman has established credit in her own name indicates that she could shop around for better deals in loans.

6.  LIABILITY, COLLISION and COMPREHENSIVE. Most states and most banks will require you to carry these types of insurance. The names may be slightly different in some states.

7.  POWER OF ATTORNEY. The durable power of attorney allows the other spouse to carry on the financial affairs and business of the disabled or sick spouse.

8.  A DEBIT card transfers funds from your account INSTANTLY whereas a CREDIT card allows you to pay with installments.

9.  32% or about 1/3 of the income to the family should be allocated to housing expenses in your budget. While it seems high, it is the figure most lending institutions use in figuring your loan.

10. FALSE. There is a 3 day cooling off period during which you can cancel door-to-door sales.

11. FALSE. This is folklore. You may date a check on any date, holidays included.

12. TRUE.

# *Your life is Big Business. Run it like one.*

You've invested a lot in your life: time, money and the prime of your life. So learn to take advantage of the tools, techniques and strategies of big business to get the greatest return on your investment.

Several years ago when Chrysler got into financial trouble, did you hear them say, *Oh poor, poor me, we just can't make it so we'll have to go under!* Did management retreat and drown itself in self-pity?

No, they didn't--and neither should you. Do you think the American public would have felt sorry for Chrysler if it had been drowning in self-pity? Then, why should you be any different?

People don't want to hear about your problems...they have problems of their own. Did you ever go to a social gathering and hear someone complaining about all their problems and how life was just so bad? Did you enjoy being around them? Was it fun?

Isn't it more fun to be around upbeat and happy people who are bubbly and who make you feel good instead of dragging you down to a lower level?

What was the first thing Chrysler did to begin its comeback?

They took inventory of what they had and what they needed. That is where you need to begin: take an inventory of your family and your assets.

*"Feelings of inferiority and superiority are the same. They both come from fear."*

# Take Inventory of Your Family

The first step in solving any problem is to learn where you are starting from. In order to do that you will have to think a little about YOU, your family, your possessions and your interests.

**Knowledge is power.**

If you will follow the simple steps in this book, you will find that you will become stronger because you will understand more about your life and your activities.

*On the next few pages are information sheets that you need to have handy at all times.* **Complete them now!**

# FAMILY STATUS INFORMATION

Husband's name: _____

Date of Birth: _____ Soc.Sec.# _____

Wife's name: _____

Date of Birth: _____ Soc.Sec.# _____
Home Address: _____

Business Address: (H) _____
                  (W) _____

## Children's Names

| and Addresses | Sex | Date of Birth | Married, Single Divorced | Soc. Sec.# |
|---|---|---|---|---|
| _____ | _____ | _____ | _____ | _____ |
| _____ | | | | |
| _____ | _____ | _____ | _____ | _____ |
| _____ | | | | |
| _____ | _____ | _____ | _____ | _____ |
| _____ | | | | |
| _____ | _____ | _____ | _____ | _____ |
| _____ | | | | |

## OTHERS TO BE CONSIDERED

| Names and Address | Sex | Birth Date | Relationship | Soc. Sec. # |
|---|---|---|---|---|
| _____ | _____ | _____ | _____ | _____ |
| _____ | _____ | _____ | _____ | _____ |
| _____ | _____ | _____ | _____ | _____ |
| _____ | _____ | _____ | _____ | _____ |
| _____ | _____ | _____ | _____ | _____ |
| _____ | _____ | _____ | _____ | _____ |

# VITAL STATISTICS (female)

The information below will be necessary for completion of various documents and announcements should anything happen. Complete it NOW for future reference. Should a death occur simply make a photocopy of this page and give to the Funeral director.

Date_____

My full name _____
First          Middle          Last

Address_____
City        State        County

Birthplace _____
City        State        County

Birthdate_____

Citizen of what country_____ Naturalization No._____

Usual occupation _____

Social Security Number _____

Industry or Business _____

If Veteran, name of war(s) _____

Dates of Service _____

Branch of service and rank _____Serial # _____

Year residence established in this state _____

Year residence established in this community _____

Marital status:  Married_____Single ___Divorced ___Widow_____

Name of husband _____
Birthplace _____Date_____
City        State        County

Name of father _____
Birthplace _____Date_____
City        State        County

Mother's maiden name _____
Birthplace _____ Date _____
City        State        County

# VITAL STATISTICS   (male)

The information below will be necessary for completion of various documents and announcements should anything happen. Complete it NOW for future reference. Should a death occur simply make a photocopy of this page and give to the Funeral director.

Date_____

My full name _____
              First          Middle          Last

Address _____
              City           State           County

Birthplace _____
              City           State           County

Birthdate _____

Citizen of what country_____   Naturalization No._____

Usual occupation _____

Social Security Number _____

Industry or Business _____

If Veteran, name of war(s) _____

Dates of Service _____

Branch of service and rank_____Serial #_____

Year residence established in this state _____

Year residence established in this community_____

Marital status:    Married ____Single____Divorced____Widower____

Name of wife _____
Birthplace _____Date _____
              City           State          County

Name of father _____
Birthplace _____Date _____
              City           State          County

Mother's maiden name _____
Birthplace _____ Date _____
              City           State          County

# *Medical*

A matter that frequently arises in one's lifetime is the medical background and history of a family's illness. Doctors, hospitals, and even children and grandchildren need this information.

In addition, many women with small children often travel or are away from home or school and need to have medical information available should anything happen to their children that needs immediate attention. **In all cases** you need to sign and have available for friends, relatives, or trusted neighbors medical consent forms that authorize them to act on your behalf should anything happen to your children when you are not available.

Compete these forms NOW, make photocopies and sign each one separately, giving the copies with the original signatures to responsible people who will be willing to act for your family in your absence. It will give you peace of mind that will help in times of stress.

# FAMILY MEDICAL HISTORY

Any disease that "runs in your family" should be discussed with your doctor.

| | Father | Paternal Grandfather | Paternal Grandmother | Mother | Maternal Grandfather | Maternal Grandmother | Siblings | | | | | Spouse | Children | | | | |
|---|---|---|---|---|---|---|---|---|---|---|---|---|---|---|---|---|---|
| Allergies | | | | | | | | | | | | | | | | | |
| Amblyopia | | | | | | | | | | | | | | | | | |
| Anemia | | | | | | | | | | | | | | | | | |
| Asthma | | | | | | | | | | | | | | | | | |
| Arthritis | | | | | | | | | | | | | | | | | |
| Bladder or Kidney Trouble | | | | | | | | | | | | | | | | | |
| Bleeding Tendencies | | | | | | | | | | | | | | | | | |
| Cancer or Tumor | | | | | | | | | | | | | | | | | |
| Diabetes | | | | | | | | | | | | | | | | | |
| Epilepsy | | | | | | | | | | | | | | | | | |
| Glaucoma | | | | | | | | | | | | | | | | | |
| Gout | | | | | | | | | | | | | | | | | |
| Hearing Defects | | | | | | | | | | | | | | | | | |
| Heart Trouble | | | | | | | | | | | | | | | | | |
| High Blood Pressure | | | | | | | | | | | | | | | | | |
| Mental Illness | | | | | | | | | | | | | | | | | |
| Mental Retardation | | | | | | | | | | | | | | | | | |
| Rheumatism | | | | | | | | | | | | | | | | | |
| Stomach or Duodenal Ulcer | | | | | | | | | | | | | | | | | |
| Strabismus (Crossed Eyes) | | | | | | | | | | | | | | | | | |
| Stroke | | | | | | | | | | | | | | | | | |
| Tuberculosis | | | | | | | | | | | | | | | | | |
| Other | | | | | | | | | | | | | | | | | |
| Age at Death | | | | | | | | | | | | | | | | | |
| General Health (Good or Poor) | | | | | | | | | | | | | | | | | |
| BIRTH DATE | | | | | | | | | | | | | | | | | |

# EMERGENCY CARE CONSENT FORMS

*The information on this page is the type of information used to give permission to a hospital or doctor for treatment of you or your child in case of an emergency. This is a suggested form for you **to copy, sign** and leave with the person(s) responsible for the individual in your absence.*

## ADULT CONSENT FORM

Permission is hereby granted for the performance of any medical and surgical procedures and treatments, transfusions, diagnostic examinations, and the administration of anesthetics or drugs which are deemed advisable to save my life by a licensed physician or hospital (unless otherwise stated) to or upon me.

_____
Signature and date

Emergency Care Consent Form Location/Date_____

_____

## CHILD CONSENT FORM

Permission is hereby granted for the performance of any medical and surgical procedures and treatments, transfusions, diagnostic examinations, and the administration of anesthetics or drugs which are deemed advisable to save the life of the child by a licensed physician or hospital (unless otherwise stated) to or upon _____.
                     Child's Name

_____
Parent or Legal Guardian

Date:_____

Extra Space for instructions:_____

_____

_____

# PERSONS TO BE NOTIFIED IN CASE OF EMERGENCY

Date:_____

Name:_____ Relationship:_____

Address: _____

Telephone Number:_____

Date: _____

Name:_____Relationship:_____

Address:_____

Telephone Number:_____

## PHYSICIANS

Date:_____

Name: _____

Address:_____

Telephone Number:_____

Date:_____

Name:_____

Address: _____

Telephone Number:_____

## DENTIST

Name:_____

Address:_____

Telephone Number:_____

14

# *Things around the house YOU MUST Know!*

Everyday household items are often taken for granted. They don't often create problems so we don't worry about them. Once they do cause trouble, knowledge of their whereabouts and what to do becomes serious and immediate.

On the next pages is a checklist of everyday household items YOU NEED to know. Look over the list and complete the right hand column as you learn the location and what to do in an emergency with each one. It is very important to complete this easy section. To skip it now may someday put you and your family in a life threatening situation that you can avoid with a little effort NOW!

*Begin your journey toward self-sufficiency by learning about your own home or apartment. This exercise will enhance your knowledge of everyday items and build your self-confidence.*

There are four basic things about your home/apartment YOU NEED TO KNOW:

**(1) Location and how to use the MAIN WATER SHUT-OFF VALVE;**

**(2) Location and how to use the NATURAL GAS SHUT-OFF VALVES** (*if you use natural gas in your home*)**;**

**(3) Location and how to use the MAIN ELECTRICAL FUSE and/or CIRCUIT BREAKER BOX;**

**(4) Names and phone numbers of utilities and responsible repair services.**

On the next three pages are forms for you to complete...NOW! Get your spouse or some knowledgable person to show you these items and how to use them.

THEN, look up the phone numbers (*and emergency phone numbers*) of the various services and utilities in the phone book and record them on the forms.

(If you don't know the name of a good reputable service for your appliances, ask the recommendation of a friend or neighbor who has had experience with a particular company or individual. Lacking that, start with the store that sold you the machine or is selling the same brand that you have. It may have its own service shop, or more likely, it will give you the names of firms that do installation and repair work.)

**DO NOT PROCEED FURTHER** until you complete these first forms. *(I have given you a sample answer in the middle column of the form so you will have an idea of what to put in your notes.)*

If you live alone, call your utility services and ask them to send someone out to show you how these valves and switches work. NO, they won't think it is a dumb request. As a matter-of-fact, they will gain respect for you for asking. *(What does the Bible say about that? If you don't ASK, you don't GET!)*

*(Let me tell you a little secret...many husbands/male friends don't know the answers to these questions either and are afraid to ask!)*

IF YOU USE NATURAL GAS, it wouldn't hurt for you to make a list of all gas appliances in your house (*including your hot water heater, if it is gas*). The reason...if you ever have to turn off the main gas valve, you will need to know which units will require relighting of the pilot lights when you turn the gas back on. Get the Gas Utility representative to show you how.

# HOUSEHOLD THINGS YOU NEED TO KNOW

*The following are things every woman needs to know about the house.*

| DESCRIPTION | SAMPLE | YOUR NOTES |
|---|---|---|
| **Water Valve.** The main water valve that shuts off water coming into your house. | *Located near hot water heater with red tag marked "shut off "in garage.* | |
| **Sink Valve.** The water valves that shut off water to your kitchen and bathroom sinks. (Typically two valves--one *Hot* and one *Cold* water.) | *Located under the sink in the kitchen and bath rooms.* | |
| **Toilet valve.** The valve that shuts off water going to the toilet water tank. | *Located under the water tank behind the toilet in the bathroom.* | |
| **Electrical Power Box.** This is the main power panel for the house. It contains fuses or circuit breakers that control the electricity going to the various rooms of the house. (*Determine its location and make sure the various circuits are labeled. Your house will not have both a fuse box and a circuit breaker panel--one or the other--probably a circuit breaker box.*) | *Gray box in garage near back door with switches inside. Extra fuses, if needed, are located in bottom of box.* | |
| **Electrician.** The name and phone number of a competent and reasonably priced electrician. | *Smith Electrical Service John Smith 312 South Summer St. 555-1234* | |
| **Plumbing.** Who is a responsible and reasonable company should I have any plumbing problems? | *Ajax Plumbing Company 1546 Apex Way 555-6789* | |
| **Natural Gas Valve.** Location of gas shut off valve.(*Call local gas company to come out and teach you location and how to use.*) | *Located on gas meter outside of house.* | |

**17**

**Furnace Gas Cut-off Valve:**
Location and how to use the gas
cut-off valve.

*In basement near bottom of
furnace. Turn to off position
and be sure pilot light goes
out.*

_____

_____

**Hot Water Heater Gas Cut-off
valve:** Location and how to turn
off and relight pilot light.

*Hot water heater is in garage
and gas cut-off valve is located
just above the heater.*

_____

_____

_____

**Stove Gas Cut-off valve:** Location
and how to turn off and how to
relight the pilot light.

*My stove doesn't have a main
valve but has individual unit
valves on the stove itself.*

_____

_____

**Gas Clothes Dryer Cut-off Valve:**
Location of and how to turn off
gas supply to your gas dryer.

*The gas cut-off valve is located
in the wash room near the
water cut-off valves to the
dryer.*

_____

_____

**Fireplace chimney cleaning:**
Every chimney needs to be
cleaned periodically because of
the accumulation of resin from
burning wood on the inside of
the chimney. Get the name and
phone number of chimney
sweep in your area.

*My chimney was cleaned in
August 1988 by
Ajax Chimney Sweepers
555-8765.*

_____

_____

_____

Elephants don't bite. It is the little things that getcha! The above information sounds
very basic and simple ...and it really is, but it is often taken for granted until you need
to know it. Know the little things about your home and you will have a much better
peace of mind.

Most of the utility companies will be glad to send someone out to your house at no
charge to show you how to use their appliances. *(This is the gas company, the electric
company and the water company, not the dealer you bought the appliances from.)*
Take advantage of their service and don't be afraid to ask a lot of questions when the
service person comes out. That is the only way you will learn the things you need to
know.

Someone once said that the difference between a smart person and a wise person is
that a smart person knows everything but a wise person knows everybody. You want
to be wise and know who to call and what to do while they are on the way.

# IMPORTANT UTILITY NUMBERS

*The following is a list of your utilities and numbers that are to be called in the event of an emergency.*

**ELECTRICAL SERVICE:** _____

Telephone:_____

Emergency telephone:_____

**NATURAL GAS SERVICE:** _____

Telephone:_____

Emergency telephone:_____

**TELEPHONE SERVICE:** _____

Telephone:_____

Emergency telephone:_____

**WATER SERVICE:** _____

Telephone:_____

Emergency telephone:_____

**SEWAGE SERVICE:** _____

Telephone:_____

Emergency telephone:_____

**HEATING/AIR CONDITIONING SERVICE:** _____

Telephone:_____

Emergency telephone:_____

**PLUMBING SERVICE:** _____

Telephone:_____

Emergency telephone:_____

*"If you don't start, it's certain that you won't finish."*

# *Important Papers*

In every family, just like a big business, there are important papers that must be maintained and kept available for reference should the need arise. There are obviously many locations where these papers may be kept, and that is OK. The real question is, Where are they located?

The next page is a checklist that you and your family should complete that will give the location of these papers. Keep this list current so that should anything happen you know exactly where the papers that you need are located.

Remember, **Knowledge is Power.**

# IMPORTANT PAPERS

| DOCUMENT | LOCATION | | KEEP FOR |
| --- | --- | --- | --- |
| | Home | Safe Dep Box | |
| **1. PERSONAL** | | | |
| *Certificate of Birth* | ( ) | ( ) | *Permanently* |
| *Certificate of Marriage* | ( ) | ( ) | *Permanently* |
| *Divorce decree (order)* | ( ) | ( ) | *Permanently* |
| *Social Security Cards* | ( ) | ( ) | *Permanently* |
| *Passports* | ( ) | ( ) | *Permanently* |
| *Wills* | ( ) | ( ) | *Permanently* |
| *Death Certificates* | ( ) | ( ) | *Permanently* |
| *Military discharge* | ( ) | ( ) | *Permanently* |
| **2. FINANCIAL** | | | |
| *Bank account information* | ( ) | ( ) | *7 years* |
| *Loan Agreements* | ( ) | ( ) | *While in force* |
| *Stocks and bonds* | ( ) | ( ) | *Permanently* |
| *Government securities* | ( ) | ( ) | *Permanently* |
| *Notes due you or others* | ( ) | ( ) | *Length of note* |
| *Passbooks* | ( ) | ( ) | *While in force* |
| *Pension or profit sharing plan information* | ( ) | ( ) | *Permanently* |
| *Other items* | ( ) | ( ) | |
| **3. TAXES** | | | |
| *Past returns* | ( ) | ( ) | *7 years* |
| *Canceled checks* | ( ) | ( ) | *7 years* |
| *Other* | ( ) | ( ) | |
| **4. INSURANCE** | | | |
| *Life Insurance policies* | ( ) | ( ) | *Permanently* |
| *Homeowners policy* | ( ) | ( ) | *1 year* |
| *Auto policy* | ( ) | ( ) | *1 year* |
| *Major Medical Health* | ( ) | ( ) | *1 year* |
| *Other* | ( ) | ( ) | |
| **5. REAL ESTATE** | | | |
| *Trust deeds* | ( ) | ( ) | *Permanently* |
| *Real estate notes* | ( ) | ( ) | *Permanently* |
| *Title policy* | ( ) | ( ) | *Permanently* |
| *Mortgage documents* | ( ) | ( ) | *Permanently* |
| *Tax assessments* | ( ) | ( ) | *7 years* |
| *Rental agreements* | ( ) | ( ) | *3 years* |

| | | | | |
|---|---|---|---|---|
| Rental receipts | ( ) | ( ) | 3 years |
| Receipts for repairs | ( ) | ( ) | 3 years |
| Receipts for improvements | ( ) | ( ) | Permanently |
| Other | ( ) | ( ) | |

## 6. MEDICAL

| | | | |
|---|---|---|---|
| Records | ( ) | ( ) | Permanently |
| Receipts | ( ) | ( ) | 1 year |
| Insurance payments | ( ) | ( ) | 1 year |

## 7. AUTOS

| | | | |
|---|---|---|---|
| Registration | ( ) | ( ) | Until sold |
| Ownership | ( ) | ( ) | Until sold |
| Loan Agreement | ( ) | ( ) | 3 years |
| Loan payment records | ( ) | ( ) | 1 year |
| Repair records | ( ) | ( ) | 3 years |

## 8. SAFE DEPOSIT BOX LOCATION

The safe deposit box where these items are located is at :_____
and is box number:_____. The names of those authorized to open the
box are:_____
_____. The key is located:_____
_____.

OR

Tape
Safety
Deposit
Key
Here

*"You can only have two things
in life, Reasons or Results.
Reasons don't count."*

# Get a Safe Deposit Box

Many of your private papers need to be kept in a location that is away from the house in the event the house is destroyed or damaged. A good location is a safe deposit box in a local bank or financial institution. It will cost you about $25 a year or so, but is well worth the small cost.

*(Incidentally, the fact that you keep the valuables in a safe deposit box will lower your insurance rates.)* But don't obtain the box in an individual's name. If something should happen to the individual, the bank may be required to seal the box.

*So what do you do?*

Open the box in a company name...a company that consists of you and a friend or your spouse. Call it something like: L & E Enterprises (for Larry and Eloise) or whatever name you choose. Use your Social Security number for the bank records, but be sure the box is in your *company* name.

No, you don't have to do any business to open a safe deposit box. The name is the key. Don't use your or your spouse's name or your last name for the box. This way you can get into it anytime.

Rent the safety deposit box at a bank or financial institution that is convenient to you and your family. Be sure that more than one person is on the signature card and can get into the box should anything happen to you. They should either have a key or know where the key to the lock box is located.

Put the information on the safe deposit box number and location on the *IMPORTANT PAPERS* document in this book for future reference.

# KEEP THE FOLLOWING IN YOUR SAFE DEPOSIT BOX

( )  Your birth certificate

( )  Naturalization papers, if you have any

( )  Marriage certificates: which may be needed to establish claims for payments from Social Security or other pension plans.

( )  Your passport, unless you use it frequently

( )  Locations of all banks and savings and loan accounts

( )  If you're divorced or widowed, divorce decree or death certificate

( )  If you're a military veteran, retirement orders and discharge papers

( )  Annuities and to whom they are payable

( )  Real estate holdings and deeds.

( )  Car title

( )  Homeowners insurance policy

( )  Stock certificates and bonds

( )  Loan Contracts

( )  Government securities

( )  Trust documents

( )  Insurance policies

# Open a JOINT Bank Account for Family Funds

If family funds are in a bank account in a husband's name alone, that money is not available to the wife when the death of the husband occurs. The banks know before your distant relatives that your husband has died, and the checks and bills come trailing back along with the first sympathy card: *"Party deceased; funds frozen."* In the case of a JOINT ACCOUNT, you won't have this problem. The bank often doesn't know anything has changed, until you tell it.

**Be sure your family bank account is a JOINT ACCOUNT.**

When opening a joint account, remind the bank that it is to be an *"or"* account and not an *"and"* account. The difference is that in an *"or"* account either of the parties can sign a check or withdraw funds; whereas, in an *"and"* account, both parties must sign for release of funds.

Also, tell the bank to begin numbering the checks with the number 2001.*(Stores are advised not to take personal checks with low numbers. It has been determined that about 87% of all bad checks begin with numbers under 500. To keep from being embarrassed, start your checks with a large number.)*

The joint account doesn't necessarily have to be with your spouse. It can be with the kids or with a trusted friend.

Reminder: NEVER open a bank account under only one person's name. Should something happen to that person, it is very difficult to obtain the funds that may be needed immediately. The second person's name doesn't have to be on the check, only the signature card.

This joint account should be in addition to your own personal bank account that will be discussed in the next step.

*"There is no way to know
before experiencing."*

# *Open Your OWN Bank Account*

It is always a good idea to have at least two people eligible to sign checks in any account. That could be your spouse or a trusted friend or relative. That way should anything happen to you, someone will be able to have access to the funds for necessities.

---

**Open your own bank checking account with your money NOW if you don't already have one.**

**Ask the bank what is the lowest deposit you must maintain in order to not be charged a monthly service charge. Then deposit at least that amount in the account. Put the rest in a savings account or a money market account.**

**Be sure it is in your own name, your LEGAL name: Mary B. Jones, not Mrs. William Jones.** *(Use a trusted friend or relative on the signature card with you.)*

---

Why?

It will give you experience in dealing with banks and in balancing your checkbook and the knowledge that you have funds for emergencies, should the need arise. You want to use your own name on the account so that you can begin to establish credit and a good track record of bill payment in your name. Also, learn what most people don't know--how to save money.

# How Long Will Your Savings Last?

Now that you have opened up your bank account and deposited some money in it or purchased a C.D., the question now arises: *If I live on it and the interest it makes, how long will the money last?*

Answer: It depends! It depends on how much you withdraw. Let's assume that you inherit or retire with $100,000. You deposit that sum in an interest bearing account. Look at the chart below to determine how long the money will last as you draw it out.

| Annual Withdrawal | Years Your Money Will Last If It Is In An Account That Makes This Much Interest | | | | | |
|---|---|---|---|---|---|---|
| | 5% | 6% | 7% | 8% | 9% | 10% |
| $6,000 | 36 | Ind.* | Ind. | Ind. | Ind. | Ind. |
| $7,000 | 25 | 33 | Ind. | Ind. | Ind. | Ind. |
| $8,000 | 20 | 23 | 30 | Ind. | Ind. | Ind. |
| $9,000 | 16 | 18 | 22 | 28 | Ind. | Ind. |
| $10,000 | 14 | 15 | 17 | 20 | 26 | Ind. |
| $11,000 | 12 | 13 | 14 | 16 | 19 | 25 |
| $12,000 | 11 | 11 | 12 | 14 | 15 | 18 |

*Ind. *means the money would last indefinitely.*

For example, suppose you need $10,000 a year to live on and your money is earning 8% interest in some account. Then your money would last for 20 years.

If you lived only on the interest of the money you have invested, your money would last indefinitely. It is when you start using a part of the initial deposit that begins to reduce the length of time the money would last.

Try to live on the interest only. You can make arrangements for the financial institution where you have the money deposited send you monthly interest payments for your living expenses.

# *While at the Bank...*

While you are in the bank there are two more steps you must take.

1. **Obtain a $50 TRAVELER'S CHECK or even two $20's. Put the check(s) in your purse and keep it there for emergencies. They are not dated and will be good until you cash them.** *(This little security idea will give you peace of mind knowing that you will always have some accessible cash available.)*

2. **Learn about the various banking services that are available to you. Any employee will be happy to explain these to you.** *(A basic list appears on the next few pages for your reference.)*

When dealing with banks use the Bible's method of learning: "ASK and ye shall receive, seek and ye shall find, knock and the door will be opened unto you." There is no such thing as a Dumb question! The only dumb question is the one you don't ask.

Before we get much further, it would be a good idea to review the various bank accounts that are routinely available to you. Here is a quick basic outline:

### 1. Regular checking accounts
    A. Minimum balance required (usually $300) or else you are charged a service charge.
    B. You receive no interest on your deposit.

### 2. Interest-bearing checking account
    A. Low interest paid on balance deposited.
    B. Minimum balance required, below which you are charged a fee.

### 3. Moneymarket checking accounts
    A. Often goes under different names, but procedure is same.
    B. More interest paid than other accounts
    C. Larger minimum balance required than other types-- usually about $2,500. If you fall below that level, you will be paid lower interest.

*(Hint: If you are writing a lot of checks each month, write the checks from your regular checking account and feed the regular checking from your money market interest bearing account as needed.)*

### 4. Money Market Mutual Funds
    A. Really not bank accounts because they are managed by stock brokerage firms.
    B. For the same money available in a hurry, comparable or higher interest rates are paid than in checking accounts.
    C. Some require a minimum balance of $500-$2,500.
    D. **NOT FEDERALLY INSURED**
    E. Brokerage houses offer several funds with different features. *(For example, Merrill Lynch has 6 different funds.)*

### 5. Savings Accounts
    Passbook account *(low interest and few benefits)*.

*(Hint: If you do use one, be sure that it compounds interest **DAILY** from the day of deposit to the day of withdrawal.)*

### 6. Trust Account
    A. You can open this type of account "in trust for" someone (usually a child) who receives the money at your death or at some other predetermined time.
    B. You pay taxes on the interest and you can change the beneficiary (person to receive the funds) and close the account at any time.

### 7. Custodial Accounts
A. This is similar to a trust account except that the beneficiary pays taxes on the interest.
B. Beneficiary is legally entitled to all the funds in the account.
C. You can't change the beneficiary.
D. You can't close the account.
E. If you are putting money aside for your children, a custodial account is useful for transferring assets out of your higher-taxed estate.
F. As custodian, you can invest a custodial account in a Certificate of Deposit (C.D.) rather than a lower interest passbook account.

### 8. Certificate of Deposit
A. Similar to a savings account, but you are required to leave it in the bank for a set period of time.
B. The longer the period, the higher the interest.
C. You can withdraw the earned interest, but you will be charged a penalty on early withdrawal of the money you deposited.

*(Hint: Don't put all your money into a C.D. Keep some in a checking account or small savings account for emergencies.)*

This gives you a basic overview of the various banking accounts that are available to you at most banks. The names may vary from area to area but the operation is essentially the same.

*Where is the best place to keep my money?*

At the place that will give you the best deal. Check all the area banks, Savings and Loan Associations, and Credit Unions. Shop around, you will be surprised at the difference in services and charges.

Remember that, in principle, you should always be looking for the highest possible interest on **ALL** your deposits, both checking and savings, plus the convenience you need to make bill paying as simple as possible.

CAUTION, not all banks and financial institutions insure your money! In all instances, *check to be sure that your money is insured* by the U.S. Government. In most financial institutions your funds are insured up to $100,000. If you have more than that, open several different accounts for not more than $100,000 in each account.

Ask your local bankers about their services. Explain that you want to possibly open a new account or accounts and would like to know more about their services. I assure you that they will take time to carefully explain everything. Don't be afraid to ask if you don't understand something.

*"You are the only teacher
you will ever have."*

# Get a Copy of your CREDIT REPORT

The day will come when you need to establish credit in your own name. The first step is to review a copy of your present credit report, if any, so that you will know what the banks and lending institutions know about you.

Remember, **Knowledge is Power.**

Follow the check list on the following pages to obtain and review your credit report. If you don't understand the report, go by the credit bureau where you obtained the copy, and they will be happy to explain it to you. ASK!

# CHECKLIST FOR YOUR CREDIT FILE

( ) Ask your local banker or a local retail store for the name and phone number of the credit bureau that they use for reports. *(They are also listed in the "Yellow Pages" of many city phone books under "Credit Bureau.")*

( ) Contact that bureau or bureaus and request a copy of your personal report. They may have their own form, or you may want to use the sample request letter in this section.

( ) When you receive your copy read over the entire credit report and make sure it is accurate.

( ) If the bureau doesn't have a report on you, write the credit bureau and ask that a file be opened in your name and that all future account activity be reported in your name a well as that of your husband.

( ) Learn the nature and substance of all the information in your file.

( ) Find out the name of each of the businesses (or other sources) that supplied information on you to the reporting agency.

( ) Learn the names of everyone who received reports on you within the past six months (or the last two years, if the reports were for employment purposes).

( ) Request that the reporting agency reinvestigate and correct or delete information that was found to be inaccurate, incomplete or obsolete.

( ) Follow up to determine the results of the investigation.

( ) Ask the reporting agency, at no cost to you, to notify those you name who received reports within the past six month (two years, if for employment purposes) that certain information was deleted.

( ) Write an explanation of any problem that appears in the report, and request that your version of the facts be placed in your file if the reinvestigation did not settle the dispute.

( ) Request the reporting agency to send your statement of the dispute to those you name who received reports containing the disputed information with the past 6 months (two years, if received for employment purposes).

( ) If you have a letter or explanation placed in your credit file, order a new Credit Report in about 2 months to be sure they put your letter in the file.

( ) Be sure to keep copies of all of your correspondence.

# REQUEST FOR CREDIT FILE DISCLOSURE TO CREDIT BUREAU

*Complete the letter below and send to your nearest credit bureau or to TRW, Inc. P.O. Box 271, Parsippany, New Jersey 07054. Include a check for $10 with your request.*

Date: _____

Credit Bureau

_____

_____

Gentlemen:

Please find enclosed my check or money order in the amount of **$10.00**.

Please obtain and forward to me my current credit **reports. I have** completed the information requested.

Name:_____

Address:_____

City:_____ State:_____ Zip: _____

Previous Address:_____

City:_____ State:_____ Zip:_____

Date of birth:_____

Social Security Number:_____

Spouse's Social Security Number:_____

If you have any questions concerning this request **my phone number where** I can be reached during the day is (___)_____-_____.

Thank you for your help in this matter.

Sincerely,

_____
(Signature)

37

## SPECIAL NOTE WOMEN CONCERNING CREDIT

*Most women know that they may apply for credit in their own name. However, most women do not know that credit applied for with their husband is recorded only in the credit file of her husband. After divorce or death of the husband, the woman has no credit file. To have credit reported in both names, use the following form, photocopied and then personalized and mailed to creditors with which you hold a joint account such as Sears, American Express, Visa, MasterCard, etc. Send to the address on your monthly credit statements.*

_____
(Date)

_____
(Name of Creditor)

_____
(Address of Creditor)

_____
(City)          (State)          (Zip)

Dear Sir or Madam:

Under the provisions of the Equal Oportunity Credit Act, I request that the credit information on the account of the undersigned be maintained in separate files, under each name. Further, I ask this information be made available to all credit reporting agencies.

I would appreciate your confirmation of this request.

Thank you very much for your time and consideration.

Sincerely,

_____
(Husband)

_____
(Wife)

_____
(Our Account Number)

# *Establish CREDIT in Your Own Name*

The day will come soon when you need some extra money. You will need credit to borrow money. Don't wait until you need it to try to establish credit. The time to establish credit is when you don't need any money.

Credit is granted on a lender's confidence that the borrower will repay. Therefore, the lender usually checks your credit history with one or more of the credit bureaus that collect data about a person's bill paying practices and debts. These bureaus don't rate you; they simply report what they learn from subscribing stores, banks, and credit card issuers. They also have limited responsibility for accuracy.

To establish credit, you must borrow something and repay it. For those with no credit history, the best way is to set up a savings account, then take out a passbook loan with the savings acting as collateral.

Credit card companies will often let young borrowers start with an account cosigned by their parents. A cosigner may be the answer too for older people who have always paid with cash. The Equal Credit Opportunity Act sets a special "user" category that could help women with accounts in their husbands' name to build a credit record. Ask for an ECOA/TYPE account or loan.

Follow the checklist on the next page to establish credit.

# CHECKLIST FOR ESTABLISHING CREDIT

( ) Open a bank account in your own name. Make sure it is your legal name (*your legal name may be Sue Jones, Sue B. Jones, or Mrs. Sue Jones; it is **not** Mrs. Bill Jones.)*

( ) Request that your checks begin with the number 2001.

( ) It is generally a good idea to have two signatures on the signature card at the bank for your account. Be sure the second person's name does not appear on your checks.

( ) Pay your household bills from your personal account. Put the utilities and telephone in your legal name using initials for your first and middle names or at least in joint names with your husband, but pay those bills out of your personal account. *(Use S.B. Jones, not Sue B. Jones on your utility accounts. It will eliminate a lot of crank telephone calls.)*

( ) Get credit and/or charge cards in **your own name,** even if you and your husband already have joint cards. (If you can't get a card in your own name, have your husband or parent co-sign for you. Then after one year, request that the co-signer be released, since by then you will have established a credit worthy payment record.)

( ) Take out a loan from the bank or credit union in your name...even if you don't need the money. Make the loan a small one...say $1,000 or so. You can put the money from the loan in a savings account that pays you interest which you can then use to repay the loan 2 or 3 days before the loan is due.

( ) Ask the loan officer for the minimum time you can borrow the money to establish credit. That will determine the time of the loan. In many cases that period is a minimum of one year. Always pay the loan before due. (Try to borrow the money for 1 year.) If necessary have your husband or parent co-sign for the loan with you.

( ) What if you have no one to co-sign your loan? No problem! Simply place an amount of money equal to the loan you want in a savings account at the same bank, and tell the banker you want to use that money in the savings account as your collateral. It can even be the same account where you will keep the money you borrow. They will nearly always accept that for collateral for the loan. *(Incidentally, collateral is the item or money that you pledge to the bank to secure the money you borrow. If you don't pay them back, they can sell the item or transfer the money from your account to pay off the note. Collateral is a kind of insurance for the bank.)*

( ) Ask for a signature loan, that is, one without collateral. If the bank is unable to loan you money based solely on your signature, don't feel offended. That simply means that since you don't have a credit history with them, you must establish one before they can loan you money on your signature alone.

( )  Be able to answer the following questions when applying for a loan:
    1. How long have you lived in the area?
    2. How long at your present address?
    3. Do you own or rent?
    4. Do you have a telephone, savings account or investments?
    5. What is your occupation?

( )  If the bank asks you whether or not you want Credit Life insurance on the loan, your answer is NO! Credit Life insurance is simply insurance on your life with the bank named as the one (also called a beneficiary) to receive the proceeds from the policy should anything happen to you. Your note would then be paid off. It is not a good deal!

( )  On your next major purchase (auto, furniture, etc.) buy on time, then after 1 year pay it off if you can.

( )  Quick review for credit: First, get in the habit of paying your bills on time. Second, establish a bank account. Manage the account carefully so that your checks never bounce. Third, open charge accounts at one or two local stores. Fourth, borrow a little money even if you don't need it.

## IF YOU HAVE CREDIT PROBLEMS

*If you're notified you don't qualify for credit or that credit is denied for any reason, take these steps:*

1. Call the person who signed the letter to make sure that no mistake was made.

2. Request in writing the reason for the denial.

3. If you receive a poor credit listing, find out the name of the reporting agency from the people of whom you are seeking credit--by law they must tell you.

4. Ask the reporting agency for a copy of your credit report.

5. If you have established good credit with a department store, bank or elsewhere, ask them for the names of their credit agencies. Contact those agencies for their favorable credit report on you and forward it to the bank or company that has denied you credit.

6. The Fair Credit Reporting Act is helpful in keeping your credit records current and complete. Among the rights you have under this Act are the rights to review your credit file at any organization during normal business hours and the right to know who received your credit report. You may correct any information in your credit report, remove adverse information after 7 years, and sue a reporting agency for damages.

# How Credit is Extended

Credit is extended for two major reasons. First, credit is extended to increase sales. Merchants know that more sales will be made when the need for ready cash is eliminated. Secondly, credit is extended to make money. Stores, banks, and finance companies show a profit from the interest they charge when you use their charge accounts.

In issuing credit, two factors are used to determine your "credit worthiness." First, your ability to repay the credit which is extended is determined. This will include your job, length of employment, position, etc. Secondly, your past credit history is examined...your *credit report.*

Credit history is considered to be more important than your ability to repay any credit extended. The best references are major bank credit cards, travel and entertainment cards, and major department store cards. These cards reflect major purchasing power. Steady repayment over time is considered the ideal credit condition. Credit extended over the last three years is the most reliable indication of credit activity.

**Things to remember** when requesting credit are: (1) Have a phone in your name or one you can use on your applications; (2) it is always good to have at least six months or longer on your present job; and (3) you should be earning over $150 per week.

Keep in mind that when applying for credit it is always best to visit the bank, department store, or finance company IN PERSON. Always look your best. Appropriate attire for women is a conservative dress, not slacks. Always speak with confidence and always appear truthful and trustworthy. Do not appear to be nervous or sloppy. Never be in a rush to get your money and get out.

*REMEMBER: what credit rating you have already established is now being reported, and what you choose to do now will be reported in the future.*

**TO HELP YOU** create a good impression when making a credit application, we have prepared a series of forms on the next few pages that YOU MUST complete before visiting a bank or credit card company. By completing these now and taking them with you to the financial institutions you will be in control because you will have all the information they will need to extend you credit. If you don't complete them NOW, you will have to complete similar forms at the bank before they will extend you credit.

# CHECKLIST FOR MEETING WITH FINANCIAL INSTITUTION

Name of Institution: _____

Meeting date: _____

| ITEM | SOURCE OF INFORMATION | CHECK IF INCLUDED |
|------|----------------------|-------------------|
| **Copy of Income Tax Returns** | | |
| 19_____ | _____ | ( ) |
| 19_____ | _____ | ( ) |
| 19_____ | _____ | ( ) |
| **Financial Statements** | _____ | ( ) |
| **Budget Estimates** | _____ | ( ) |
| **Copy of Will** | _____ | ( ) |
| **Copy of Trust Agreement** | _____ | ( ) |
| **List of all Real Property** | _____ | ( ) |
| **Other** | _____ | ( ) |

43

# BANK CHECKLIST

| NAME OF BANK | ADDRESS | ACCOUNT # | TYPE |
|---|---|---|---|
| _____ | _____ | _____ | _____ |
| _____ | _____ | _____ | _____ |
| _____ | _____ | _____ | _____ |
| _____ | _____ | _____ | _____ |
| _____ | _____ | _____ | _____ |

## LIST OF STOCK

| Name of Security | No. Shares | Owner | Current value |
|---|---|---|---|
| _____ | _____ | _____ | $ _____ |
| _____ | _____ | _____ | $ _____ |
| _____ | _____ | _____ | $ _____ |
| _____ | _____ | _____ | $ _____ |
| _____ | _____ | _____ | $ _____ |
| _____ | _____ | _____ | $ _____ |

## BOND SECURITIES

| Type | Owner | Interest Rate | Due Date |
|---|---|---|---|
| _____ | _____ | _____ | _____ |
| _____ | _____ | _____ | _____ |
| _____ | _____ | _____ | _____ |
| _____ | _____ | _____ | _____ |
| _____ | _____ | _____ | _____ |

# ASSETS

date_____

## CASH

| | |
|---|---|
| Money on hand | $_____ |
| Balance in checking account(s) | $_____ |
| Balance in savings account(s) | $_____ |
| Balance in Money Market accounts | $_____ |

## SECURITIES

Stock Market Investments $_____

Bonds $_____

U.S. Savings Bonds $_____

Mutual funds $_____

Other investments (CDs, Govt securities, etc) $_____

**Cash Surrender Value of Life Insurance** $_____

**Notes Receivable** $_____

**Real Estate** $_____

**Autos and Other Vehicles** $_____

**Pension and/or Profit-Sharing Funds** $_____

**Individual Retirement and Keogh Accounts** $_____

## OTHER ASSETS

Home furnishings and household goods $_____

Jewelry, furs, and silver $_____

Art and antiques $_____

Other personal property $_____

Other items _____

_____ $_____

**TOTAL ASSETS** $_____

# LIABILITIES

date_____

**ACCOUNTS PAYABLE** *(what you owe to others)*

Charge cards ............................................ $_____
Credit cards ............................................ $_____
Medical bills ........................................... $_____
Utilities .................................................. $_____
Alimony and child support .................... $_____
Other_____ $_____
_____ $_____
_____ $_____

**CONTRACTS PAYABLE**

Automobiles ............................................ $_____
Furniture ................................................ $_____
Installment credit contracts .................. $_____

**NOTES PAYABLE TO OTHERS**

Banks ...................................................... $_____
Real estate mortgages .......................... $_____
Others_____ $_____
_____ $_____

**TAXES**

Property taxes ........................................ $_____
Federal taxes ......................................... $_____
State Taxes ............................................. $_____

**TOTAL LIABILITIES** $_____

**TOTAL ASSETS**           $_____
**-TOTAL LIABILITIES**   - $_____
 **NET WORTH**      =      $_____

46

# DEBTS OWED TO US
as of _____

| DESCRIPTION | TERMS | BALANCE | LOCATION OF DOCUMENT |
|---|---|---|---|
| _____ | _____ | $ _____ | _____ |
| _____ | _____ | $ _____ | _____ |
| _____ | _____ | $ _____ | _____ |
| _____ | _____ | $ _____ | _____ |
| _____ | _____ | $ _____ | _____ |
| _____ | _____ | $ _____ | _____ |
| _____ | _____ | $ _____ | _____ |

# DEBTS WE OWE

*Here is an explanation of some long-term obligations which are not a normal part of our monthly budget:*

| Description | Terms | Balance | Location of Document |
|---|---|---|---|
| _____ | _____ | $ _____ | _____ |
| _____ | _____ | $ _____ | _____ |
| _____ | _____ | $ _____ | _____ |
| _____ | _____ | $ _____ | _____ |
| _____ | _____ | $ _____ | _____ |
| _____ | _____ | $ _____ | _____ |
| _____ | _____ | $ _____ | _____ |
| _____ | _____ | $ _____ | _____ |
| _____ | _____ | $ _____ | _____ |
| _____ | _____ | $ _____ | _____ |

# REAL ESTATE PROPERTIES

As of _____

| Property Address | Description<br>1. Home<br>2. Vacation Home<br>3. Commercial<br>4. Industrial<br>5. Residential Investment | Approximate Value | Holder of Loan |
|---|---|---|---|
| 1. | | | |
| 2. | | | |
| 3. | | | |
| 4. | | | |
| 5. | | | |

48

# *Obtain a CREDIT CARD*

**To obtain credit, if you have no credit record at all, start small.**

If you have a job, seek a small line of credit by going to a local bank or credit union and requesting a $300-$500 line of credit on a VISA or MasterCard. They will supply you with the necessary forms for application for the card.

If the banks are too large in your area to make this small credit line, try instead to get a credit card at a local department store.

Do not try to open too many accounts at one time. Credit bureaus keep a record of each creditor that inquires about you. Some creditors may deny your application on the grounds that you are trying to open too many accounts and may exceed your ability to pay them.

If you must start with a card from just one local store, you might also apply for a card from a nationwide gasoline company. They tend to be easier to get than the bank cards. Use those and any card you get wisely, and before you know it, the banks will be trying to loan you money with your established credit.

*What if you have no job and no income other than insurance or alimony, how do you obtain a credit card?*

If that is the case, the best way to start is to go to a credit union or small bank and ask for a small loan as I mentioned previously. They may insist on collateral (such as a car, or money in a savings account) to offset the loan. Do it once, pay off the loan on time, and you'll have no trouble getting the second loan if you ever need it, or the "plastic" (slang for credit cards) you want.

**If you are turned down --DON'T GIVE UP!**

First, ask to speak with the credit manager or bank loan officer. Explain face-to-face why you are a good credit risk. Lenders look at three things when considering whether or not to make a loan. The lender first looks at your *ability to pay,* and they also look at what you *own* that may be used as collateral for the loan. Finally the lender tries to judge your *reliability* or *willingness to repay*. Knowing this, explain to the banker or lending officer why you meet all of those criteria.

If that fails to work, try another bank or store. Different banks and stores have different criteria for grading credit risks.

Be sure to check your Credit Report to be sure it is accurate before talking with the banker. Remember, you can make corrections in the report, and you definitely want to know what it says before he sees it so you can explain any adverse information that may be contained within the report.

How many credit cards should you carry?

That will obviously depend upon your spending habits and your self control. However, a good rule of thumb is to carry at least a Visa or MasterCard and one other card. Many places don't accept all cards. If you travel often, you might want to consider an American Express card. With that card you can get cash should you get into a bind. That card is more difficult to obtain than many other cards, however.

Why obtain bank cards instead of just store cards?

Bank cards have the advantage of be being *multi-purpose* as compared with single purpose store cards. In other words, you can use the MasterCard or Visa cards at a multitude of stores, restaurants, theaters, airlines, hotels, etc. If you think about it, you'll see the great advantage of being able to use a single card at all those establishments, instead of having a separate card for each.

**Too much credit** may be an unexpected problem in having too many credit lines, even if you use them wisely. When you apply for a new form of credit, the new lender-to-be may pay more attention to the total of your existing credit lines than to what you actually borrow on them.

For example, let's say that you have several bank and retail cards, with credit limits that total $10,000, though you only owe less than $1,000. If you now apply for an auto loan or a home mortgage, the new lender may count your present debt as $10,000 rather than $1,000, since you *could* borrow up to $10,000 on your cards without applying for any additional approval.

Moral: it may be unwise to carry credit lines far above what you actually need. If you find yourself at a disadvantage with a new lender because of the situation we've just described, show the lender how you've actually used your cards and see what you can work out.

# *Learn to USE a Credit Card*

Once you've established your right to credit and credit cards, how should you use it? Specifically, how much should you use it?

Use the credit cards only for the purpose of not having to carry a lot of cash with you at all times.

Before we talk about a credit card you should know the difference between a DEBIT card and a CREDIT card. A DEBIT card looks like a Credit card but it behaves very differently. A good example of a DEBIT card is the one the bank issues you to withdraw funds from your account through an automatic teller machine. Put in the card, punch in your identification number and you can withdraw or deposit funds directly into your account INSTANTLY.

Therein lies the big difference! Funds are transferred *instantly* with a Debit card! With credit cards, you don't pay until the end of the month or whenever you receive the statement from the card company.

Just make sure you know which card you have!

The checklist on the next page is a good one to follow when using credit cards.

# CHECKLIST FOR CREDIT CARD USE

( ) Go to your bank and fill out a request for a Visa or MasterCard bank credit card. Bank cards have the advantage of being *multi-purpose* as compared with single purpose store cards. In other words, you can use the MasterCard or Visa cards at a multitude of stores, restaurants, theaters, airlines, hotels, etc.

( ) When you receive your credit card, put the number of the card, the expiration date, and the number to be called if it is lost on the form on the next page. Then sign the card on the space provided on the back. *(This will force anyone trying to use your card to forge your signature...often quite difficult.)*

( ) **When using credit cards, treat them as if you were using CASH!**

( ) Pay the **entire** credit card bill off EVERY MONTH when it comes in. No Exceptions. If you pay off the entire balance, you pay no interest at all on that month's purchases. Remember that you are paying 21-27% interest on any money that you don't pay off on credit card purchases each month.

( ) Keep all charge receipts in an envelope at home. Compare these receipts with the charges on your credit statements when you get them. Notify the credit card company of any errors. Do so immediately!

( ) NEVER use your credit cards to buy anything that is not in your budget for the month or for anything on impulse.

( ) When you purchase anything with a credit card, always ask for and get the carbons of the credit purchase. Then YOU destroy the carbons. *(If the carbons reach the hands of a thief, the thief can use the information to mail order or telephone order thousands of dollars worth of merchandise to be charged to you.)*

( ) Adopt this rule: **The first month you are unable to pay off the credit card charges ENTIRELY, the card(s) will be destroyed.**

( ) Once you have obtained credit in your own name, I would suggest that you CUT UP all of your credit cards except perhaps one for emergencies. That will discourage you from running up your credit card bill--which is very easy to do.

( ) **If you lose or have your cards stolen or find that someone has used them without your permission, take the following action:**

    1. **Call the credit card company office immediately** *(remember you recorded the number on the form in this section)* **and report the problem.**

2. **Make a note of the person's name you talked with and the date and time of the call.**

3. **Immediately write the credit card company to confirm the phone call.** *(Send to the address for billing errors not necessarily where you send your monthly payments.)*

4. **Tell them which charges are unauthorized; and/or the date the card was discovered missing. Point out which signatures on the sales receipts are wrong.**

5. **The Fair Credit Billing Act limits your liability to a maximum of $50 for unauthorized use of the credit card no matter how much the thief has charged** *provided,* **you notify the credit card company in writing as soon as you discover the loss or unauthorized use.**

( ) Do not buy the credit card protection service that you may receive information on in the mail. You don't need it!

( ) Limit the number of cards that you carry. Generally all you need is a multi-purpose card such as Visa or MasterCard and perhaps an oil company card for gas. If you travel very much you may want to take an American Express travel card. But in any event, no more than 3 cards will be needed.

( ) Beware of phone calls offering you exotic prizes, vacations and club memberships that ask for your name, credit card number and expiration date. If you give this information, you have in effect, given away your credit card.

( ) Whenever possible pay for car and home repairs with your credit card. The reason is that, should the repairs not be correct, you can notify the credit card company, who will simply not pay the repair service until you are satisfied.

( ) NEVER, repeat, NEVER lend your card to anyone else.

( ) **Avoid trouble** with your credit cards. You should worry seriously about your situation if :

1. The money you owe is steadily rising.
2. You are only making the minimum required payments.
3. The amount you owe is getting close to your credit limits.
4. You are carrying a large number of charge accounts and/or credit cards with large amounts of money owed on all or most of them.
5. You are taking cash advances to meet regular living expenses.
6. You are delaying payment of month-end bills because your checking account is too low.

If any of these descriptions applies to you, take these steps:

1. Stop using new credit.  Cut up your cards...NOW!
2. Go back to your budget and work on it until you have worked out a plan to reduce your total debt month by month. You will have to cut expenses, but DO IT.

---

**The CARDINAL RULE of successful financing:**
*Stay out of debt beyond current monthly expenses!*

---

(   ) If you do fall hopelessly behind and owe everyone and the milkman, then after cutting up the cards take a bank loan and pay off everything at once.  The banks charge lower interest rates than the credit card companies, and you preserve your image as a responsible, bill-paying, adult human being.

(   ) *Remember a credit card is to a compulsive spender what one drink is to an alcoholic.*

(   ) Complete the following chart NOW with your present credit cards and add any new ones to it as you receive them.

## Credit Cards

| Name of Card | Card # | Expiration | Phone if lost |
| --- | --- | --- | --- |
| _____ | _____ | _____ | _____ |
| _____ | _____ | _____ | _____ |
| _____ | _____ | _____ | _____ |
| _____ | _____ | _____ | _____ |
| _____ | _____ | _____ | _____ |
| _____ | _____ | _____ | _____ |
| _____ | _____ | _____ | _____ |

# Wise Buying Checklist

*When wondering whether you should or should not buy, give yourself this quiz and find out.*

|  | YES | NO |
|---|---|---|
| 1. Do you really need this item? | ( ) | ( ) |
| 2. Is the price reasonable? | ( ) | ( ) |
| 3. Is this the best time to buy the item? | ( ) | ( ) |
| 4. If this is a bargain, is it a current model? | ( ) | ( ) |
| 5. If "on sale" is the price a true sale price? | ( ) | ( ) |
| 6. Are you sure no less expensive item can be substituted? | ( ) | ( ) |
| 7. Arc you sure there are no major disadvantages? | ( ) | ( ) |
| 8. If cost is too high, will it truly satisfy an inner need? | ( ) | ( ) |
| 9. Have you checked and researched the item? | ( ) | ( ) |
| 10. Do you know the store's reputation? | ( ) | ( ) |
| 11. Does the retailer offer any special services with the item? | ( ) | ( ) |

## Scoring:

9-10 Yeses------Buy the product.

6-8  Yeses-----think again.

less than 6-----forget it.

*" Trying provides two excuses,
an excuse for not Doing, and
an excuse for not Having."*

# *Make a BUDGET*

Every successful business, every succcessful athletic team, and every successful person makes a *written* plan...a kind of game plan...and so should you!

In order to make ends meet, you have to plan ahead, and you do so by budgeting your expenditures. In this portion of the course, you must make a budget, using the rules I have set out here.

In preparing a budget, it is important that you base it on a *monthly* rather than an annual basis. On the next few pages there is a monthly form to guide your budget preparation.

The percentages referenced here are not absolute and will vary with income and geographical location but are based on recommendations by highly respected financial counselor Larry Burkett.

This is perhaps the main step in gaining financial self-sufficiency. It is easy to skip making a budget, but just remember that when you do you will defeat the purpose of this entire book. So complete the budget immediately after reading this material. You can do it!

Below is a suggested budget guideline for your monthly income and expenses. Read through these guidelines and then complete the forms that follow. A Sample budget appears immediately after the guidelines.

## A. Housing (32% of take home pay)

Typically, this is one of the largest home budget problems. Many people buy a home they can't afford, motivated by peer pressure or some other pressure. It is not necessary for everyone to own a home. The decision to buy or rent should be based on needs and financial ability rather than internal or external pressure. See the How Much House Can I Afford chart below. It will give you a good idea as to how much you can afford.

# HOW MUCH HOUSE CAN I AFFORD?

*(Using the budget on the next few pages the question arises, how much can I afford to spend on a house and make the payments? We have prepared a table below that will help you to quickly determine your ability to make the payments.)*

For example: Suppose you take home $36,000 a year in your job. That is $3,000 a month. Now assume that the current mortgage interest rate is 10% per year. Looking at the chart below, we find that the house price that you can afford is $119,000.

As a general rule you can estimate the monthly house payment, including insurance and taxes to be about 1% of the cost of the house. In this case if you bought a $119,000 house and financed 80% or about $95,200, your monthly payments would be about $952 per month or a little less.

| Monthly Income | Annual Percentage Rate | | | | | | | | | | |
|---|---|---|---|---|---|---|---|---|---|---|---|
| | 8.00% | 8.50% | 9.00% | 9.50% | 10.00% | 10.50% | 11.00% | 11.50% | 12.00% | 12.50% | 13.00% |
| $7,000 | $312,000 | $301,000 | $291,000 | $283,000 | $272,000 | $263,000 | $255,000 | $247,000 | $239,000 | $232,000 | $225,000 |
| 6,000 | 268,000 | 259,000 | 250,000 | 242,000 | 234,000 | 226,000 | 219,000 | 212,000 | 206,000 | 199,000 | 193,000 |
| 5,000 | 225,000 | 217,000 | 209,000 | 202,000 | 196,000 | 189,000 | 183,000 | 177,000 | 172,000 | 167,000 | 162,000 |
| 4,000 | 181,000 | 175,000 | 169,000 | 163,000 | 157,000 | 152,000 | 147,000 | 143,000 | 138,000 | 134,000 | 130,000 |
| 3,000 | 137,000 | 132,000 | 128,000 | 123,000 | 119,000 | 115,000 | 111,000 | 108,000 | 104,000 | 101,000 | 98,000 |
| 2,000 | 94,000 | 90,000 | 87,000 | 84,000 | 81,000 | 78,000 | 76,000 | 73,000 | 71,000 | 69,000 | 66,000 |

*Assumes you pay ⅓ of take-home pay in housing costs and the bank lends you 80 percent of the value of the house.

## B. Food  (15% of take home pay)

Most people buy too much food.  Others buy too little.  Typically, the average American family buys the wrong type of food. The reduction of a family's food bill requires quantity and quality planning.

---

### Hints for Grocery Shopping:

- Always use a written list of needs.
- Try to conserve gas by buying food for a longer time period and in larger quantities.
- Avoid buying when hungry.
- Use a pocket calculator, if possible, to total purchases.
- Reduce or eliminate paper products--paper plates, cups, napkins, etc.  (Use cloth napkins.)
- Evaluate where to purchase sundry items such as shampoo, mouthwash, etc. (These are normally somewhat less expensive at chain drug stores.)
- Avoid processed and sugar-coated cereals. (These are expensive and of little nutritional value.)
- Avoid prepared foods, such as TV dinners, pot pies, cakes, etc. (You are paying for expensive labor.)
- Determine good meat cuts that are available, from roasts or shoulders, and have the butcher cut these for you.
- Try house-brand canned products. (These are normally less expensive and just as nutritious.)
- Shop for advertised specials.
- Avoid buying non-grocery items in a grocery. supermarket except on sale.  (These are normally "high mark-up" items.)
- *Leave the children at home* to avoid unnecessary pressure.
- Check every item as it is being "rung up" at the store and again when you get home.

---

## C. Automobiles  (15% of take home pay)

The advertising media refers to us as "consumers" but that's not always the best description. I believe that P.T. Barnum had a more apt word--suckers. Often we are unwise in our decision-making when it comes to our machines-- especially cars.

Many people will buy new cars they cannot afford and trade them long before their utility is depleted. Those who buy a new car, keep it for less than 4 years, and then trade it for a new model have wasted the maximum amount of money. We swap cars because we want to...not because we have to. Don't  forget to budget in maintenance and oil changes.

## D. Debts (**5**% of take home pay)

It would be great if most budgets included 7% or less for debts. Unfortunately, the norm in American familes is far in excess of this amount. As previously discussed, credit cards, bank loans and installment credit have made it possible for families to go deeply into debt. What things can you do once this situation exists?

1. Destroy all of your credit cards as a first step, if you can't pay off the entire amount each month.

2. Establish a payment schedule that includes all creditors.

3. Contact all creditors, honestly relate your problems, and arrange a fair repayment plan.

4. Buy on a cash basis and sacrifice your wants and desires until you are out of debt.

## E. Insurance (**5**% of take home pay)

It is unfortunate to see so many people misled in this area. Few people understand insurance, either how much is needed or what kind is necessary. Almost no one would allow someone to sell her a Rolls Royce when she could only afford a Chevrolet; yet many people purchase high cost insurance when their needs dictate otherwise.

Insurance should be used as a supplementary provision for the family, not protection or profit. An insurance plan is not designed for saving money or for retirement.

In our society, insurance can be used as an inexpensive vehicle to provide future family income and thus release funds today for family use.

One of your best insurance assets is to have a trustworthy agent in charge of your program. A good insurance agent is usually one who can select from several different companies to provide you with the best possible buy and who will create a brief, uncomplicated plan to analyze your exact needs.

## F. Recreation-entertainment (**7**% of take home pay)

We are a recreation-oriented country. That is not necessarily bad if put in the proper perspective. But those who are in debt cannot use their creditor's money to entertain themselves. Be careful to stay within this range for your entertainment expenses.

## G. Clothing (**5**% of take home pay)

Many people in debt sacrifice this area in their budget because of excesses in other areas. Yet, with prudent planning and buying, your family can be clothed neatly without great expense.

Do your purchases reflect good utility rather than ego?

Do you buy clothes to satisfy a need or desire?

Do you have a closet full of clothes you no longer wear because they are "out of style"?

## H.  Medical-dental expenses ( **5**% of take home pay)

You must anticipate these expenses in your budget and set aside funds regularly; failure to do so will wreck your plans and lead to indebtedness. *Don't be afraid to ask doctors or dentists in advance about costs.*

In the case of prescriptions, shop around. You will be amazed to discover the wide variance in prices from one store to the next.

## I.  Savings  (**5**% of take home pay)

It is very important that some savings be established in the budget. Otherwise, the use of credit becomes a lifelong necessity and debt a way of life. Your savings will allow you to purchase items for cash and shop for best buys, irrespective of the store.

Saving a portion of your take home pay is also good discipline for you, and the money you save will come in handy in the event of an emergency. You need to have in a savings plan at least enough money to cover 3 months of your regular living expenses should anything happen...**3 months**!

---

### SAVINGS HINTS

**Use a company payroll withdrawal, if possible.**
**Use an automatic withdrawal from your checking account.**
**When an existing debt is paid off, reallocate that money to savings.**

---

## J. Variable household expenses.  (Miscellaneous) (**6**% of take home pay)

One of the most important factors in home expenses is ...**YOU**. If you can perform routine maintenance and repair, considerable expenses can be avoided. If every hour of the day is tied up in the pursuit of money, you are in bondage. A part of care and maintenance around the home relates to family life, particularly the training of children. When they see you are willing to do some physical labor around the house, they will learn good habits. But if you refuse to get involved, why should they?

Where will they ever learn the skills of self-sufficiency?

---

### BUDGET HINTS

If you get a raise or a gift of money or any unlooked for, unexpected income, pretend you didn't. Don't spend it. Put it into your savings account.

If you have a bank loan or an installment payment, don't stop making payments after you've paid it up. Just put the same amount regularly into your savings account.

Shop for groceries right after a meal when you are not hungry. Stick to your shopping list.

Don't carry credit cards with you. Or, if you feel you must, try leaving them at home one week a month. See if you don't spend less money. Also, go to the bank and get a $20 or a $50 traveler's check and keep it with you at all times for an emergency...it is no good to anyone else and gives you some peace of mind.

Try saying NO for a week. No chocolate bars, no magazines, no movies, no wine, no splurging.

Every purchase should be evaluated as follows:

*Is it a necessity? Have I assessed whether it is a need, a want or a desire?*

*Is this the very best possible buy I can get or am I purchasing only because I have this credit card?*

*Does it require costly upkeep?*

---

As a single in this time of economic instablity, you must get out of debt altogether if possible.

Let me define debt. Debt exists with any of the following conditions:
(1) Payment is past due for money, goods or services that
     are owed to other people.
(2) The total value of unsecured liabilities exceeds total assets.
     In other words, if you had to cash out at any time, there
     would be a negative balance on your account.

Anxiety is produced in the area of financial responsibility when the family's basic needs are not being met.

When in debt, avoid the use of what is called "leverage." Leverage is the ability to control a large asset with a relatively small amount of invested money. That sounds good and it may be, but not if you are already in debt.

For example, if you bought a piece of property that cost $10,000 and required $1,000 down, that represents a 9 to 1 lever. You have invested 10% of your money and borrowed 90%.

Borrowing money to invest is not smart nor wise for anyone. When you invest and borrow money from a bank to do so, the repayment of the bank loan is dependent on the investment making a profit. But if a profit is not made and the investor can't make the payments, he loses the investments and still owes the bank. The result? Financial bondage.

Look at the next few pages and complete them NOW. Yes, it takes a little time, but if you want to be secure and self-sufficient YOU MUST prepare a BUDGET.

The next question that I often receive is, *How do I calculate the percentages?*

It is very easy. Let's say that your take home pay is $30,000 a year. To find the amount you should budget for your household expenses, 32%, simply multiply the $30,000 X .32 (32% =.32). That will give you $9,600. That amount is the amount you should budget for the household for the YEAR. Divide that by 12 (months), and you arrive at the monthly figure of $800. See, it isn't hard.

# MONTHLY BUDGET GUIDE

**Income per month**

| | |
|---|---|
| Salary | $_____ |
| Interest | _____ |
| Dividends | _____ |
| Notes | _____ |
| Rents | _____ |

**TOTAL:**  $_____

**Gross Income**

**Less:**

**1. Religious tithe**  — _____

**2. Tax**  — _____

**INCOME:**  $_____
Net Spendable

**3. Housing  *32%**  $_____

| | |
|---|---|
| Mortgage | _____ |
| Insurance | _____ |
| Taxes | _____ |
| Electricity | _____ |
| Natural Gas | _____ |
| Water | _____ |
| Garbage Pick-up | _____ |
| Telephone | _____ |
| Maintenance | _____ |
| Other | _____ |

**4. Food  *15%**  $_____

**5. Automobile (s) *15%** $_____

| | |
|---|---|
| Payments | _____ |
| Gas & Oil | _____ |
| Insurance | _____ |
| License | _____ |
| Taxes | _____ |
| Maint./Repair/ Replacement | _____ |

**6. Insurance  *5%**  $_____

| | |
|---|---|
| Life | _____ |
| Medical | _____ |
| Other | _____ |

**7. Debts *5%**  $_____

| | |
|---|---|
| Credit Card | _____ |
| Loans & Notes | _____ |
| Other | _____ |

**8. Entertainment & Recreation  *7%**  $_____

| | |
|---|---|
| Eating Out | _____ |
| Trips | _____ |
| Babysitters | _____ |
| Activities | _____ |
| Vacation | _____ |
| Other | _____ |

**9. Clothing  *5%**  $_____

**10. Savings  *5%**  $_____

**11. Medical Expenses *5%** $_____

| | |
|---|---|
| Doctor | _____ |
| Dentist | _____ |
| Drugs | _____ |
| Other | _____ |

**12. Miscellaneous  *6%**  $_____

| | |
|---|---|
| Cosmetics | _____ |
| Beauty/Barber | _____ |
| Laundry/cleaning | _____ |
| Allowance/Lunch | _____ |
| Subscriptions | _____ |
| Gifts (incl. Christmas) | _____ |
| Special Education | _____ |
| Cash | _____ |
| Other | _____ |

**TOTAL EXPENSES**  $_____

**Net Spendable Income**  $_____
**Less Expenses**  — _____

****Total (Deficit/Surplus)** $_____

*Percentage of net spendable income.
**This total should break even or show a surplus.

64

# SAMPLE BUDGET

*Below is a sample budget prepared based on an annual income of $20,000 using the suggested percentages in the budget plan on the previous page. Your income will obviously vary from the figures given here, but this will serve as a guideline for your budget planning.*

## THE FAMILY BUDGET GUIDE

**INCODE PER MONTH** _____

Salary _____
Interest _____
Dividends _____
Notes _____
Rents _____

**TOTAL GROSS INCOME**    $1667

Less:
1. Tithe    −120

2. Tax    −300

**NET SPENDABLE INCOME**    $1247

3. Housing    *32%    400
  Mortgage (rent) _____
  Insurance _____
  Taxes _____
  Electricity _____
  Gas _____
  Water _____
  Sanitation _____
  Telephone _____
  Maintenance _____
  Other _____

4. Food    *15%    187

5. Automobile(s)    *15%    187
  Payments _____
  Gas & Oil _____
  Insurance _____
  License _____
  Taxes _____
  Maint/Repair/
   Replacement _____

6. Insurance    *5%    63
  Life _____
  Medical _____
  Other _____

7. Debts    *5%    63
  Credit Card _____
  Loans & Notes _____
  Other _____

8. Enter. & Recreation    *7%    $87
  Eating Out _____
  Trips _____
  Babysitters _____
  Activities _____
  Vacation _____
  Other _____

9. Clothing    *5%    63

10. Savings    *5%    63

11. Medical Expenses    *5%    63
  Doctor _____
  Dentist _____
  Drugs _____
  Other _____

12. Miscellaneous    *6%    75
  Toiletry, cosmetics _____
  Beauty, barber _____
  Laundry, cleaning _____
  Allowances, lunches _____
  Subscriptions _____
  Gifts (incl. Christmas) _____
  Special Education _____
  Cash _____
  Other _____

**TOTAL EXPENSES**    $1251

**INCOME VS. EXPENSE**

Net Spendable Income    $1247
Less Expenses    −1251
**Total (Deficit/Surplus)    ⊖4

⊖4

* Percentage of net spendable income.

** This total should break even or show a surplus. If total expenses are greater than net spendable income you must cut back on expenses. Percentages for fixed and variable expenses may be adjusted but total should not exceed net spendable income.
Discipline in following your budget will produce financial freedom in your home.

# CONSUMER RIGHTS QUIZ

*Test your ability to take care of yourself in today's market place, your awareness of important consumer rights, by answering this consumer rights quiz. True or False:*

1.  Mail order firms generally must fill orders within 30 days or offer your money back.　　　　　　　　　( ) True　( ) False

2.  Parents and students over 18 have the right to see most school records and get inaccurate information corrected.　( ) True　( ) False

3.  All wearing apparel selling for more than $3.00 is required to carry care labels.　　　　　　　　　( ) True　( ) False

4.  There is a 30 day cooling off period on door-to-door sales contracts.
    　　　　　　　　　( ) True　( ) False

5.  If your credit card is lost or stolen, you are liable for any amount until you notify the issuer.　　　　　( ) True　( ) False

6.  If you complain about an error in your bill to a creditor and don't hear from them for 2 months, you are entitled to keep the disputed amount up to $50, whether or not an error has been made.　　( ) True　( ) Flase

7.  The Fair Credit Collection Practices Act prohibits anyone from harassing or abusing you, calling you repeatedly at odd hours, or telling anybody other than you that you owe money.　　( ) True　( ) False

8.  With a few exceptions, no law prevents a private organization from demanding your Social Security number, but no law says you have to provide it either.
    　　　　　　　　　( ) True　( ) False

9.  The Federal Wage Garnishment law limits the amount of your wages that your employer may withhold to repay a creditor to whom you owe money.
    　　　　　　　　　( ) True　( ) False

10. If you have overpaid or returned an item and forgot you have credit outstanding, the store can pocket the money after 30 days.
    　　　　　　　　　( ) True　( ) False

---

*Answers: (1) True; (2) True; (3) True; (4) False, there is a 3 day cooling off period during which you can cancel door-to-door sales; (5) False, you are liable for up to $50 provided you notify the card company; (6) True; (7) False. It applies only to debt collectors who regularly collect money for others, not the creditor or his attorney; (8) True; (9) True; (10) False. You must be sent a refund or a notice of your credit during each billing period.*

# How to Buy a NEW CAR

You've decided to buy a car. You are terrified. You've never ventured alone into an automobile dealer's showroom and don't have a brother or uncle who's a car nut to go with you. You've heard all the horror stories and are totally befuddled by all the talk of rebates, trade-ins, factory invoices, 1.9 percent financing and warranties.

Fear not. You don't have to be a mechanic in order to buy a car. Take a few simple steps before you sit down with any automobile salesperson, and you'll be able to negotiate like a pro and the get the car you want, with the service you need, for a decent price.

Remember--***Knowledge is Power***.

The purchase of a car represents the second largest expense most people see in their lifetime. Therefore, it is important for you to plan for the purchase...just like you did when you bought your home or rented your apartment. Buying a car is much like buying a house. *Everything is negotiable.*

On the next page is a checklist that you should follow when considering buying a new car.

# BUYING A NEW CAR CHECKLIST

( ) Before you begin, understand that EVERYTHING about buying a car is negotiable...much like buying a house. You don't buy a car like you buy a MacDonald's hamburger.

( ) Visit several different new car dealers, and test drive several different models in your price range. Pick up literature on the model while you are there. Tell the salesperson you intend to buy a car BUT NOT until you've seen and test driven several different models from several different dealerships.

( ) Ask questions about the car. Remembering that the only DUMB questions are the ones you DON'T ask. This is a fact finding trip, not a purchasing trip. Don't discuss price, just talk about your needs in a car.

( ) After you've shopped around a little, go by any bookstore and pick up some magazines on automobiles and read about the models you like. (Hint: *Consumer Reports* devotes its entire April issue each year to automobile reviews.)

( ) After you have visited several dealerships and done your reading, select TWO (2) cars you like. It is VERY IMPORTANT to select 2 cars.

( ) Once you have selected the two possibilities (preferably from different dealers) go to any public library or bookstore and pick up a copy of the latest *Edmund's New Car Prices* book. See what your selected new cars and the options you want actually cost the dealer. *(This is a VERY IMPORTANT step.)*

( ) Next go to your bank and talk with a loan officer about the car you want, what options and what kind of financing the bank can offer you. Ask for 48 and 60 month payment schedules. *(You need this information as a basis of comparison with dealer financing plans that you will check into later.)* While at the bank, ask the loan officer to check his NADA Blue Book for the value of your present car.

( ) Call another bank or credit union to see what interest rates and terms they are offering on a new car loan.

( ) You are ready to buy you new car when:
   1. You have picked and test driven two cars you like.
   2. You know exactly what the dealers paid for them.
   3. You know what your old car is worth.
   4. You know what terms a bank will give you on a new car.
   5. You have checked the reputation of the local dealers.

( ) Now call several dealers and ask for prices on the model you want with the options you want. Tell them you are price shopping. Check with dealers up to 50 miles away. *(Sometimes you can get better deals from smaller more rural dealerships.)*

( ) Next walk into a car dealer, tell the salesperson you are prepared to buy a new car. Tell him exactly the make, model and style that you want and the exact options you want on it.Tell the salesperson you have a low price on that model from another dealer and see if he will match it or come close. *(Don't talk trade-in or financing---only price.)*

( ) Dealers make their profit on the options. So ask the dealers to remove any unwanted options. If they refuse, simply be prepared to walk or drive to the next dealer. *(Remember you picked at least two different cars you wanted.)* The fact that you can leave the car deal there and walk away gives you POWER.

( ) Since you know what the approximate cost to the dealer is, you can add about $250 to that cost and make an offer. *(They won't take your first offer and really cry in their beer about the deal. That's OK as that is part of the game being played.)*

( ) Stick to your guns. Don't let them talk you up more than a few hundred dollars and only then after arguing some. If they try, simply thank them and be prepared to walk out. Once they see you know what you are talking about, they will work out a suitable deal with you.

( ) When you make an offer, be sure they include sales tax, registration, license plates, and make-ready in the deal.

( ) Don't buy the "protection packages" or extended warranty packages that will be offered. You don't need them in most cases. These are big profit items for the dealer and very little help to you.

( ) After you agree on a price, then ask the dealer what kind of loan he can offer. Compare it with the bank financing by asking the following questions:
  *(1) What down payment is required?*
  *(2) What is the monthly payment ?*
  *(3) What is the length of the loan?*
  *(4) Is there a rebate and can it be applied to the down payment?*
  *(5) What is the total interest paid over the life of the loan?*

( ) Now after agreeing on a price and fully understanding the financing offered, ask the salesman what he would give you for your old car.

( ) You can either trade it in now or sell it yourself through ads in the paper.

( ) You now can sign the papers and take your new car.

See that wasn't too hard, and you had a good time in the process...right? Oh, you were probably a little scared at first but the more you got into it the more confidence you gained and the better you felt. See how *Knowledge is Power.*

*When is the best time to buy a car?*

There are generally two times that are better than others. The first is in August and September, near the end of the model year. The other time is in the winter, January, February, and March, when car sales are very low because of the bad weather. The dealer still has his expenses such as rent, salaries, etc., and will often sell at very good prices. The worst time, probably, to buy a new car is when the new models first come out in late September or October. There is generally a big demand for the new cars at that time and the dealers don't want to discount them very much because the demand is there.

When you start to see ads and commercials offering rebates and ridiculously low-rate financing--1.9 percent is the current headline--you know sales are slow, the inventories on the lots are high, and the buyer is in a good bargaining position.

The key to buying a new car is simply *be prepared.* Know what you want and what the dealer paid for it and the EXACT options you want. Refuse those you don't want and above all, be prepared to go to the next dealer if you don't feel comfortable with this dealer or his salesperson.

**Repairs.** While your car is under warranty, take it back to the dealer for any repairs covered by the warranty. Try to find a service station close to your home which you like, and go to it regularly. Station attendants can help you keep an eye on the car's condition. You also need to have the station change your oil every 5,000 miles. I've found from experience that a simple oil change will add many miles to the life your car. Look on the edge of the driver's side door for a sticker that tells when the last oil change took place.

Anytime a mechanic or other person tells you your car needs a repair that costs more than $100, you need to get a second opinion from another mechanic before having the work done.Always ask the price of any work before having it done, even minor things like oil changes and wheel balancing. Otherwise you may be charged exorbitantly, and if the work is already done, it's too late to say it's too much.

**Other Things to Check.**
    (1) Watch the tires for thinning places on just one part of the tire.
    (2) Have the station check your anti-freeze each September.
    (3) Check the spare tire in the trunk to be sure that it has air in it.
    (4) Put a flashlight with new batteries in the glove compartment.
    (5) Put a copy of the Automobile Accident Report form found on the pages in the *Insurance* section of the book in the glove compartment.

Think of your car as your friend. When it behaves worst, it needs attention most.

# MOTOR VEHICLES

Make _____ Year _____ Model_____

Purchased from_____

Date of Purchase_____ Price paid _____

ID/VIN Number *(very important)* _____

Sales/Trade Date _____ Price_____ Mileage_____

Car is titled in name of_____

Car is financed with _____ in the amount of $_____

**#2**

Make_____ Year_____ Model_____

Purchased from_____

Date of Purchase_____ Price_____

ID/VIN Number *(very important)* _____

Sales/Trade Date_____ Price_____ Mileage_____

Car is titled in name of_____

Car is financed with_____ in the amount of $_____

**#3**

Make_____ Year_____ Model_____

Purchased from_____

Date of Purchase_____ Price_____

ID/VIN Number *(very important)* _____

Sales/Trade Date_____ Price_____ Mileage_____

Car is titled in name of_____

Car is financed with _____ in the amount of $_____

" *Hoping and Wishing are excuses for not Doing.*"

# What about a USED Car?

It's no secret that people have long been in love with their cars. Where possible, you should consider buying a new car and keeping it for about 5 or 6 years. But unfortunately that isn't possible for everyone. The alternatives include riding a bicycle, walking, taking public transportation, OR buying a used car.

Buying a new car requires care and knowledge, but it is a cinch compared to entering the jungle of the used car. This is world of its own, loaded with frauds and misrepresentations, most of them flourishing precisely because the typical buyer is seeking to save money.

So much of the bad news. If things are all that black, why do three out of four of you purchasing cars for your personal use buy used cars rather then new ones?

Price.

What's more, the total ownership and operating expenses for a second hand auto are some 10 % to 55 % less than costs for a new car and they average about half of the new car's cost for similar use.

A good checklist for you appears on the next few pages to help you purchase a good used car. Follow the directions, and your chances of getting a good deal are increased considerably.

# USED Car Purchasing Checklist

( )  To take the greatest advantage of used car savings, buy a car that is one to three years old and keep the car for three years or longer.

( )  Stay away from the sleazy used car only dealers.

( )  Shop your dealer first.  You are buying his honesty and integrity.  Be sure he is a local dealer, one who also sells new cars, preferably the kind you intend to buy used. When customers trade their cars in, he keeps the cream puffs for resale.  The older cars and lemons are wholesaled to used car lots.

( )  Consider buying direct--either from an individual, preferably one you know, or from one of the major fleet operators.

( )  Visit several car lots close to home and test drive several different models until you find the one you like and fits your budget. Also consider visiting the local Hertz, National, Avis or other rental car agencies as they sell their well maintained cars each year.  Don't discuss price yet. You are only looking for a model and make of car at this time.

( )  Once you decide on the type and model of car, visit your banker or the local library and ask to see the *NADA Official Used Car Guide*.  This guide lists the current average retail and wholesale prices for most automobiles. It will give you a good idea as to the cost of the car you are looking for.

( )  Look at a copy of *Consumer Reports*  (from Consumers Union, 256 Washington St., Mount Vernon, NY 10550) which regularly rates used cars as well as new ones. *(Ask for most recent April and December issues.)*

( ) While at the bank, ask the loan officer for the loan value of the car you are interested in.  This will tell you how much you will need to come up with for the down payment. Armed with this information, you can now begin seriously shopping for the used car.

( ) First, locate a local electronic diagonistic center or reputable mechanic in your area or nearby town. Visit him and explain that you will be shopping for a used car and want to hire him to evaluate the car you choose before you buy it.  Inquire as to how much they will charge for the evaluation. (Typically about $25-40). Ask the center or mechanic to check the following:

   [ ]  Check the compression of each cyclinder.
   [ ]  Check the brakes and wheel bearings by removing all the wheels.
   [ ]  While the car is raised on the lift, check for engine, transmission, and rear axle leaks; a defective exhaust system, a damaged or repaired main frame, broken suspension components, and damaged tires.

74

[   ]   Get a written estimate of the cost of making any necessary repairs. *(If you want the car use this estimate as leverage in bargaining the price down.)*

(   )   Check the mileage. Most drivers average about 15,000 miles a year.  If the odometer shows much more than that, keep on looking for other cars. *(For example, if the model is a 1987 model and it is 1989, the car should have less than 30,000 miles on it.)*

(   )   With these basics passing your inspection, take the car on a "test drive" to your mechanic or diagnostic center for evaluation. A good dealer won't object. On your way to the mechanic, try it out in a variety of traffic condition: on a hill as well as on level ground.

(   )   Once you and your team are satisfied that the car is acceptable, ask the dealer if he will give you the name and address of the car's previous owner.  If they do, then call the previous owner and inquire about possible problems, defects, or advantages of the car.

(   )   Ask the dealer what warranties and guarantees go with the car. Try to get a guarantee that the dealer will pay in full for all necessary repairs within 30 days of the time you purchase the car. Remember this: *If it isn't in writing, you don't have a guarantee or warranty.*

(   )   Do not assume that because a used car bears an inspection sticker it's in good mechanical condition. *(Normally, state inspection laws cover brakes, steering, tires, horn, windshield wipers, headlights, brake lights, etc.--but the laws do NOT cover in any sense the condition of the engine or transmission.)*

(   )   Some of the fleet operators and rental car agencies are now offering warranties and even financing help, so check prices with them if one is near you.

(   )   If you buy a used car from a private individual, try to pay no more than 10 % over the wholesale price shown in the NADA book at the bank. Also try to get a money back guarantee to cover you if the car fails to live up to the way in which it was represented to you.

(   )   Before buying shop among the local lenders for the best financing terms as carefully as you shop for the car itself.  As with new car buying, do your insurance and finance shopping first and separately. *(A dealer won't hold a car without a sizable deposit while you shop for insurance and money, especially if the car is a "good deal.")*

(   )   Next, locate the make and model of car that you want and make your deal to buy it.

# QUICK REVIEW FOR USED CAR BUYING

(1)  Deal only with a respected, reliable local, new car dealer that also sells used cars.

(2)  Or, shop newspaper ads by private owners for low mileage, one-owner cars, and other pluses pinpointed on the previous pages.

(3)  Or, deal with a reputable, national fleet or rental car agency.

(4)  Resist the temptation of questionable "bargains."

(5)  Have a qualified mechanic or automotive clinic inspect any used car you are considering buying.

(6)  Read and understand any contract before you sign it.

(7)  Shop among several sources of used cars to find the best deal for you.

(8)  Try to get the longest warranty available, with the dealer responsible for paying in full for all needed repairs.

(9)  Be sure, if any recondition has been done, that the warranty spells out the details--and whether the car is guaranteed to pass state inspection.

(10) If your guarantee or warranty is not spelled out in writing, *you don't have one.*

(11) Control your emotions when shopping for a used car.

(12) Shopping pays off.

(13) Take care of your car.

(14) Our staff has prepared a detailed 6 page used car checklist.  If you would like a copy, simply write us a note at the address on the last page and include $2 to cover our mailing and copying costs.

# Obtain INSURANCE

## for yourself and your possessions

You and our family have worked hard for many years to accumulate what you have--your home, your automobile, and your personal possessions.  Whatever your age, it's not too late, or too early, to get insurance to protect what is yours.

Property insurance protects you against destruction by fire, theft, or other dangers to personal property, your home or your investment properties.  The most common property insurance policies are Homeowners, Renters or Condominum policies which not only protect your property,  but normally also include a casualty coverage called Comprehensive Personal Liability insurance. This protects you against lawsuits brought by others alleging damages or injury because of your negligence.

Health insurance protects you and your family from expensive hospital stays and doctor bills resulting from an accident or illness. You MUST have health insurance in today's society.

If you drive and have a car, you MUST also have automobile insurance.  It protects you personally and your second most expensive possession--your car.

The next few pages guides you through the needs and details of your insurance requirements.

# LIFE INSURANCE

*If you are single and have no dependents*--no children, no parents who need you to provide for them--you do not need **life insurance**.

*If you are married without children*--you don't really need life insurance unless you have a dependent spouse.

*If you have children*--whether or not you are married, you need life insurance. You need enough to pay for their living expenses through age 18 plus college expenses.

*If you are a parent homemaker,* you need life insurance. You need enough to pay for the cost of the services YOU now provide free for your children.

*You do not need life insurance on your children's lives.* They have no dependents.

Life insurance falls into two basic categories: *Cash value and term.*

*Cash value* insurance is known also as whole life, endowment, permanent insurance, or any number of other trade names. Its basic feature is that it is usually purchased for an individual's lifetime and does accumulate some cash reserve from the paid-in premium. It is very costly in terms of the actual after-death benefit.

*Term Insurance* means insurance that is sold for a determinable number of years. Most term policies do not accumulate any cash reserves and are literally insurance only. There are two kinds of term insurance: *decreasing term* and *level term.* In *decreasing term* the cost (payments) stays constant, but the face value decreases yearly. In *level term* the cost increases for the period selected, while the face value stays the same.

*Which is best?* It will depend upon your circumstances. It is something you should discuss with a financial planner before you talk with an insurance agent. If you need it, I would suggest that *level term* is better because the need for insurance in a family does not decrease at a predictable rate as the decreasing term policy does. It is also much less expensive.

*How much do I need?* That depends upon your present income and spending. Determine the income needed for your family without you and multiply by 16.6. For example: suppose the income needed for two children **without** your expenses is $5,150 per year. Multiplying $5,150 X 16.6 = $85,490 or about $85,000 is the amount of life insurance needed.

Another way is to use the life insurance rule of thumb: A family needs at least enough life insurance to cover 4 to 5 times its yearly income. More specifically, a family with an annual income of $20,000 needs a total of $80-$100,000 of life insurance.

# HEALTH INSURANCE

**Health Insurance.** If you don't have health insurance, you MUST get it. To carry no health insurance is to court bankruptcy. Health insurance is much too complex to discuss in detail here, but basically, there are three ways to get the protection you need:

(1) *Health Maintenance Organization* (HMO). For a flat annual or monthly fee, an HMO gives you access to doctors and hospitals for all your medical needs. Some HMO's may not accept individual enrollees. Check in your area.

(2) *Preferred Provider Organization* (PPO). This is a cross between an HMO and traditional fee for service care. It's designed to give you the peace of mind of prepayment, without losing the freedom of going to the doctor of your choice. Many insurance companies and organizations such as Blue Cross/Blue Shield offer PPOs as well as traditional medical insurance.

(3) *Traditional Medical Insurance.* This is the type of insurance that most people are familiar with. Under this system, you pick your own doctors and go to the hospitals of your choice. They send you or your insurance company a bill. If you pay it, you get reimbursed from the insurance company.

Before you try to buy health insurance on your own, see if there is any way you can get group coverage--it is much less expensive.

Should anything happen to your spouse *(death or divorce)*, you need to check with your spouse's employer and see if you can continue the current group health insurance coverage, provided you pay the premiums. In most cases the law, COBRA, requires the employer to continue coverage for up to 3 years *provided:* (1) you make the request within 60 days of the divorce or death and (2) you agree to make the premium payments.

**Note:** Remember that coverage ends if premiums are not paid on time.

When dealing in traditional health insurance, there are three levels you can buy to cover your medical needs:

(1) *Basic medical insurance.* This normally pays for the first $2,000 to $3,000 in hospital and doctor bills per illness.

(2) *Major medical coverage.* This is designed to pickup where the basic policy leaves off. It covers moderately long-term illness or injury by paying for just about everything prescribed by your doctor. Most major medical policies pay only about 80% of all the costs above the deductible amount. Get a policy that will pay at least $250,000 per illness and $500,000 during your lifetime.

(3) *Excess major medical or catastrophic coverage.* This is designed to start

paying after your bills reach $25,000 or more.

*What should you buy?*

If you can afford only one policy, buy a good major medical policy with as high a deductible amount as you can comfortably afford to handle.

Next, buy the relatively inexpensive excess major medical or catastrophic coverage. The basic medical insurance is very expensive unless on a group plan.

# MEDICARE/MEDICAID

If you are eligible for Social Security benefits, you should visit your local Social Security Office and look into the possibility of Medicare.

The Medicare program consists of two parts:
>*Part A: Hospital Insurance
>*Part B: Medical Insurance outside the hospital.

*See the next page for a summary of the current Medicare benefits.*

If you are eligible for Social Security benefits and are 65 or older, you are automatically covered for a portion of the Medicare insurance coverage. You are automatically covered for Part A *(even if you continue working beyond age 65 and are not drawing benefits).* If you do not qualify for Part A coverage and you are 65 or older, you can enroll on a voluntary basis by paying a monthly premium. If you do this you are also required to enroll in Part B.

Medicare is a valuable aid for senior citizens. But it does not cover everything--far from it. The basic Medicare Plan (Plan A) covers approximately 40-50% of your medical bills. If you subscribe to Part B, you might be reimbursed for another 20-25% of those bills.

**You need supplemental insurance to Medicare!**

Check with your friends who are on Medicare for the names of insurance companies that offer supplemental insurance to the Medicare benefits. But in any case YOU NEED THE EXTRA COVERAGE.

**MEDICAID.** Many people confuse the terms "Medicare" and Medicaid." Medicaid is a totally separate assistance program, administered and financed by local, state and federal governments. It is designed to assist low income people--including the aged, blind, disabled and other needy individuals. You can get additional information from your local state Department of Employment Security for Medicaid requirements and benefits..

# SUMMARY OF MEDICARE BENEFITS

| SERVICE | BENEFIT | MEDICARE PAYS |
|---|---|---|
| HOSPITALIZATION... Semiprivate room and Board, general nursing and miscellaneous hospital services and supplies. Including meals, special care units, drugs, lab tests, diagnostic X-rays, medical supplies, operating and recovery room, anesthesia and rehabilitation services. | Hospital stay regardless of the number of days of hospitalization. | All but $564 per year. |
| SKILLED NURSING FACILITY CARE...in a facility approved by Medicare. *NOTE: Skilled nursing facility care is not the same as custodial nursing home care. Medicare doe not pay for custodial nursing care.* | 150 days of care per year | All but about $22 per day (paid by you for first 8 days). All after 8 days paid by Medicare. |
| HOSPICE CARE. | Beyond 210 days of care if recertified as terminally ill. | All. |
| HOME HEALTH CARE. | Beginning in 1990, coverage extended to provide for intermittent care up to 6 days a week; daily care for up to 38 consecutive days. | 38 days. |
| MEDICAL BENEFITS. (Part B) | Medically necessary doctor services, outpatient hospital services, home health care, and various medical services not covered by Part A. | Beginning 1990 beneficiary pay $75 deductible and 20% up to $1,370.Medicare pays rest. |

# PROPERTY INSURANCE

*If you own your own home,* you must have a homeowner's policy. It protects your house and contents.

*If you rent,* you must obtain tenant's insurance to protect your belongings and your personal liability. (The landlord/owner of the property will have insurance on the building structure.)

Buy homeowner's insurance to protect yourself against a major disaster-- not an occasional broken window.

**"Fancy Things" Insurance--** *Furs, jewelry, and other valuables.* Most homeowner's policies have a limit on the amount the company will pay for valuables. For relatively little cost, you can have a "rider" policy to protect these things. Notify your insurance agent and ask him to list these "fancy things" on the "rider" or "floater" policy. This listing process is called scheduling, and it offers several big advantages over the protection provided by a basic homeowner's policy:

(1) **Increase** insurance for each scheduled item. Your regular homeowner's insurance typically insures your valuables for a certain amount---usually no more than about $2,500 for a particular item. By scheduling, you can insure each item to its actual cash value.

(2) **Payment** from the first dollar of loss so that your policy's overall deductible won't consume all or most of what you would otherwise recover on the scheduled item.

(3) **Protection** against types of losses a homeowner's policy would not otherwise insure.

(4) **Inexpensive** when compared with separate insurance on the same items.

The third point is especially important if you own fine arts (such as paintings, fine pottery, etc.) since most losses to them are from breakage, spilling, dropping or marring. Unless you schedule your valuables, your basic homeowne's policy insures them only for certain types of losses, such as fire, wind, theft or water damage.

*How much special coverage should you buy?* That will depend upon the value of the items you want to insure. The insurance company will want proof of the value of the items documented with a sales slip or an appraisal.

# IF A LOSS...

**Filing the claim**. If you should encounter a disaster, here are some tips that will help you file the claim:

(1) *Be absolutely forthright and honest in describing what happened, and the extent of the injury or loss.* Avoid any tendency to pad your own losses.

(2) *Find out whether you will need to obtain estimates for any repairs.* Find out the number of estimates you will need to submit, whether you or the company will select the contractor, exactly how the contractor is to be paid, and what happens if the contractor runs into delays and cost overruns.

(3) *Make any temporary repairs necessary,and take other steps to protect your property from further damage.*

(4) *Follow up your phone call with a written description of what happened.* Keep a copy in your own files.

(5) *In liability cases, let the insurance company handle the claim.* Do not promise the injured party that you "will pay for everything." Simply tell that person to file a claim with your insurance company.

(6) *Report any robbery or burglary to police.* Fill out a complete report for the police.

(7) *In case of fire, get a copy of the fire department's report on the cause and extent of the fire.*

(8) *File your claim as soon as possible.*

(9) *Write down everything.* Keep careful records of all correspondence between you and the insurance company.

(10) *If you are denied payment, get a written statement explaining why.* You will need this for any legal action against the company. under your personal injury protection.

Generally speaking, check with your friends for the name of a good independent insurance agent, one that is not tied to only one company. They will help determine your needs based on your income. Listen to their advice.

# Property Loss Reporting Form

Name:_____

Address: _____

Telephone:___(___)_____-_____

Date and time of Loss:_____

Kind of Loss *Fire, Theft, Vandalism)* : _____

Location of Loss:_____

_____

Description of Loss:_____

_____

_____

To Whom Reported:_____ Telephone:_____
(Police Department if a theft,)

Insurance Adjuster Assigned:_____

Telephone:_____

List of Damaged Items:

| Item Description | Value | Proof of Value (appraisal, receipts, photos, video tapes, etc.) |
|---|---|---|
| _____ | $_____ | _____ |
| _____ | $_____ | _____ |
| _____ | $_____ | _____ |
| _____ | $_____ | _____ |
| _____ | $_____ | _____ |
| _____ | $_____ | _____ |
| _____ | $_____ | _____ |

# AUTO INSURANCE

If you have a car, you need car insurance. But you don't need all of the types that are sold. Here is a brief guideline for the various coverages:

(1) *Bodily injury liability.* This is required in most states.

(2) *Property damage liability.* This pays for damage you cause to the property of others. **You need** a minimum of 100/300/50 of total liability coverage. This means the policy would pay up to $100,000 to any one person you injured, up to $300,000 for all persons injured in the same accident, and up to $50,000 for damage you caused to property.

(3) *Collision.* This pays for damage to your car caused by an accident. If your car is more than five years old, **you don't need** it unless the bank requires it. Once your car note is paid off, you don't need collision.

(4) *Comprehensive.* This pays if your car is stolen, vandalized, or damaged in a flood, fire, hurricane, or other natural disaster. If you have an old car, **you don't need** comprehensive coverage.

(5) *Medical payments.* This pays if you, your guests, or others in your family are injured while riding in your car, or are struck by a car while walking. If you live in a no-fault state, these persons would be covered.

(6) *Personal injury protection.* If you live in a state that has no-fault auto insurance, you will be required to carry PIP. This covers you and the guests in your car for medical bills, lost wages, housekeeping expenses, and funeral costs.

(7) *Uninsured motorist.* This pays for medical expenses and income lost to you and anyone in your car when you are injured in an accident caused by a hit and run driver or an uninsured driver. You need to purchase this insurance.

(8) *Miscellaneous coverage.* Not necessary because it increases your rates.

Collision policies include a *deductible,* which is the amount of the bill for an accident you have to pay before the insurance company steps into the picture. If your deductible is $100 and the repair bill comes to $99, you pay it all; if the repair bill comes to $150, you cover the first $100 and the insurance company pays the remaining $150.

One way to lower the cost of your insurance is to increase the size of the deductible, which means that you pay for the relatively small losses but remain insured against a major crash.

Shop around for your automobile insurance; you can save money. State Farm is the largest auto insurer in the country and one of the lowest in cost.

Some ways to save money on your insurance: (1) **Shop around** as insurance rates are competitive; (2) **Pay once a year** rather than monthly or quarterly.

**Problems.** If your insurance company decides to cancel your coverage, complain to your *state insurance department.* Generally speaking, they must have a reason for cancellation. Legitimate reasons include failure to pay premiums, having your driver's license suspended, and being convicted of drunk driving, speeding, or reckless driving that lead to an injury or death.

They are not permitted to cancel your coverage or raise your rates if you're in an accident that is not your fault.

**Accident.** Look on the next few pages of this book NOW and find the what-to-do-in the-case-of-an-accident form, and make a copy of it. Put a copy in the glove compartment of each of the family cars for reference, should you be involved in an accident.

**Ways to cut insurance costs.**

1. Check the rates of other insurance companies, or ask an agent to do it for you. You may be able to get the same or better coverage at a lower rate.

2. If you're eligible, join a group auto plan.

3. Cancel collision insurance on an older car that is paid for. There is not enough value in it to make the policy worthwhile.

4. Cancel comprehensive insurance (for theft and general damage) on an older car. If you want to keep it, eliminate perils such as flood and flying objects and insure only against fire and theft.

5. Take a larger deductible on collision and comprehensive insurance. This means that you pay for the small repairs yourself but are still insured against a major loss.

6. Don't buy a super-high-performance car or load it up with a lot of flashy extra accessories. Insurers will suspect that you mean to speed and charge you more.

7. Insure all of your cars with the same company in order to get their volume discount. If one of the cars is rarely driven, say so.

8. Ask about discounts for such things as car pools, a good safety record, low annual mileage, better bumpers, and compact cars. There may also be discounts for good students, students (and adults) who have taken driver education and people who don't smoke or drink.

9. Tell the insurance company about any changed circumstances that might lower your rate. for example, a married woman who finds herself single again may pay less because her husband no longer drives her car.

10. Insure a car belonging to your young son or daughter in your name, listing them as a principal driver.

# CURRENT INSURANCE POLICIES

for the year_____

| Insurance for: | Insurance Co. | Policy No. | Expires |
|---|---|---|---|
| **AUTOS**<br>*(Liability, Fire, Theft, Collision)* | _____ | _____ | _____ |
| **RESIDENCE** | | | |
| *(Building)* | _____ | _____ | _____ |
| *(Contents)* | _____ | _____ | _____ |
| *(Second Home)* | _____ | _____ | _____ |
| **LIABILITY TO OTHERS**<br>*(Non-auto)* | _____ | _____ | _____ |
| **EXTRA LIABILITY LIMITS**<br>*(Personal Umbrella)* | _____ | _____ | _____ |
| **MEDICAL AND SURGICAL** | _____ | _____ | _____ |
| **MAJOR MEDICAL** | _____ | _____ | _____ |
| **LIFE INSURANCE** | _____ | _____ | _____ |
| | _____ | _____ | _____ |
| | _____ | _____ | _____ |
| **DISABILITY** | _____ | _____ | _____ |
| **OTHER** | _____ | _____ | _____ |
| | _____ | _____ | _____ |

# Insurance Beneficiary Worksheet

| Name | Relationship | Total Amount of Money I want them to have | Specific Assets I want them to have |
|------|--------------|-------------------------------------------|--------------------------------------|
| _____ | _____ | _____ | _____ |
| _____ | _____ | _____ | _____ |
| _____ | _____ | _____ | _____ |
| _____ | _____ | _____ | _____ |
| _____ | _____ | _____ | _____ |
| _____ | _____ | _____ | _____ |
| _____ | _____ | _____ | _____ |
| _____ | _____ | _____ | _____ |
| _____ | _____ | _____ | _____ |
| _____ | _____ | _____ | _____ |

Use this form when you review the family's future cash needs and the insurance requirements. Take time to consider how much money and what particular assets you want to leave to other people. You can use this worksheet in preparing your will as well as evaluating your insurance needs.

When considering life insurance policies, remember that the owner of the policy is the person responsible for paying the premiums, and not necessarily the one who is insured.

# ACCIDENT REPORTING FORM (AUTOMOBILE)

(Keep this form in the car)

## Accident Information

Date:_____ Time:_____
Location:_____
_____
Brief description of accident:_____
_____
_____
_____
_____

## Other cars Involved:

Driver's name:_____
Address:_____
Telephone: (        )_____
Driver's license number:_____State:_____
Auto Make:_____Year:_____Type:_____Color:_____
Registration number:_____State:_____
Owner of Auto:_____
Address:_____
Telephone: (        )_____
Their insurance company or agency:_____
_____

## Passengers or Other Persons Injured

Name:_____Address:_____
_____
Name:_____Address:_____
_____

## Witnesses

| Name | Address | Telephone |
|------|---------|-----------|
| _____ | _____ | _____ |
| _____ | _____ | _____ |
| _____ | _____ | _____ |
| _____ | _____ | _____ |

*Police Officer Who Took Report*
*Name:*_____*Badge Number:*_____

*Report number:*_____

*Diagram of accident:*

## IN CASE OF ACCIDENT:

**1. Be Careful** what you say to others involved. Don't misrepresent your part, but also, don't make promises or say more than is necessary. Statements you make can be used against you in court.

**2. Identify witnesses.** Since many cases end up with the parties blaming each other, a third-party witness can be helpful. Bystanders often wait to be asked. Get names, addresses and phone numbers.

**3. Document the accident** in the space above.

**4. Observe carefully.** It's hard to believe, but some accidents are "set up" and you may be the fall guy. If anything seems odd, tell the insurance adjuster.

**5. Watch how the other party acts.** Some people are animated at the accident scene--bending, stooping, moving freely--with no sign of physical distress. Later they claim terrible injuries. What you observe could be important.

**6. Report the accident** to your insurance carrier, immediately.

# POWER OF ATTORNEY

Did you ever wonder who would take care of your financial affairs if you were suddenly hospitalized? Unless you and your spouse share ownership of bank checking and savings accounts, your family could be left without access to funds held in your name only.

To avoid such a situation, you need to execute a Power of Attorney so that he or she can act in your place if you are unable to do so. It doesn't have to be your spouse, it could be a son or daughter that you trust implicitly.

Both you and your spouse, if alive, should sign a Power of Attorney NOW, authorizing the other to handle your affairs should anything happen to you or him. This should be done now even before a Will is drawn up or signed. See your attorney or use the form on the next two pages until you can see your attorney.

A Power of Attorney is a kind of supplement to a Will in that it gives each of you broad powers without further action on anyone's part and is good for use in times of serious illness. A Power of Attorney form appears on the next page. Once you sign separate (one for you from him and one for him from you) keep them in a safe place until you need them.

The law requires that you put a Power of Attorney in writing and that you sign it before a notary public; otherwise anyone could claim to act on your behalf.

A Power of Attorney can be revoked at any time by a simple written statement referencing the original Power of Attorney and indicating your intent to revoke same.

If you hold a Power of Attorney and need to sign a check or other document, sign it with the other person's name, then your name and the phrase *"Attorney in fact."*

*"What you are afraid to do
is a clear indicator of
the next thing you need to do."*

# POWER OF ATTORNEY

BE IT HEREBY KNOWN THAT I, the undersigned _____

a citizen of and living at _____ do

appoint my_____,of _____to serve

as my true and lawful attorney for me, and in my name:

1. To make deposits, to endorse checks, promissory notes, and to make deposits in any and all accounts, both savings and checking in any bank in which I have any such account.

2. To withdraw funds from any of such checking accounts and savings accounts by check or withdrawal drafts.

3. To have access to any safe deposit boxes which I have or may rent in my name in any bank in the United States.

4. To accept, endorse, cash, and deposit all pension checks coming to me from any source whatsoever.

5. To enter and take possession of any land and/or buildings that may belong to me.

6. To collect and receive any rents, and all profits of any such lands or part of such lands and/or buildings that may be due me.

7.To pay all sums of money that may be hereafter owned by me in whatever just claims.

8. To execute and perform any act, deed, matter or thing whatsoever that ought to be done in relation to any and all property owned by me in my best interests.

In the event of my said attorney-in-fact shall die or become incapable of

acting as my attorney-in-fact, I hereby appoint my_____

of_____to be my attorney-in-fact in place of _____

_____, with power of exercise all of any of the powers

and authorities hereinbefore conferred on said _____.

*continued on next page*

And I, the said _____, do hereby ratify and confirm all whatsoever my said attorney shall do, or cause to be done, in or about the premises, by virtue of this Power of Attorney.

IN WITNESS WHEREOF, I have hereunto set my hand on this ____day of _____, 19____.

_____

**WITNESSES:**

_____

_____

**NOTARY:**

Sworn to and subscribed before me this _____day of _____,19____.

_____
Notary Public

My Commission expires:_____

*Note:* This power of attorney is made out naming one of your children or a trusted friend to carry out your affairs in case some debilitating illness makes it impossible for you to carry on your affairs.

# LIVING WILL

Many people who do not wish to have their life prolonged when death is imminent have a "Living Will" prepared. A Living Will is a document that is made while you are alive and which states your permission to be allowed to die without medical or surgical treatment and that you do not want the use of life support machines to sustain you in the event of terminal illness. It requires two witnesses and is recognized by many states.

A Living Will form appears on the next page.

*"Worry comes from the belief that you are powerless."*

# Living Will

I,_____, willfully and voluntarily make known my desire that my dying shall not be artifically prolonged under the circumstances set forth below, and do hereby declare:

If at any time I should have a terminal condition and my attending physician has determined that there can be no recovery from such condition and my death is imminent, were the application of life-prolonging procedures be withheld or withdrawn, and that I be permitted to die naturally with only the administration of medications or the performance of any medical procedure deemed necessary to provide me with comfortable care or to alleviate pain.

In the absence of my ability to give directions regarding the use of such life-prolonging procedures, it is my intention that this declaration shall be honored by my family and physician as the final expression of my legal right to refuse medical or surgical treatment and accept the consequences of such refusal.

I understand the full import of this declaration and I am emotionally and mentally competent to make this declaration. In acknowledgment whereof, I do hereinafter affix my signature on the _____ day of _____,19_____.

_____
Declarant

## WITNESSES

We, the subscribing witnesses hereto, are personally acquainted with and subscribe our names hereto at the request of the Declarant, an adult, whom we believe to be of sound mind, fully aware of the action taken herein and its possible consequence.

We the undersigned witnesses further declare that we are not related to the Declarant by blood or marriage; that we are not entitled to any portion of the estate of the Declarant upon his/her decease under any will or codicil thereto presently existing or by operation of the law then existing that wer are not the attending physician, an employee of the attending physician or a health facility in which the Declarant is a patient; and that we are not a person who, at the present time, has a claim against any portion of the estate of the Declarant upon his/her death.

_____      _____
Witness                                                    Witness

## NOTARY

Subscribed, sworn to and acknowledged before me by_____,
the Declarant, and Subscribed and sworn to before me by_____
and _____, witnesses, this _____ day of _____, 19_____.

_____
My Commission Expires:_____      NOTARY PUBLIC

*"If you are not leaning,
No one will ever let you down."*

# YOU Need A WILL!

Do you have a will? If not, you have probably given some thought to it. You know it is a good idea to make a will, but one thing or another keeps coming up, and you put off doing something about it.

*Do I really need a will?*

YES! Pure and simple--even if your husband is still alive and has one, you need to have your own will.

Most people die without a will, because they don't have a clear idea as to the law and how their property will be distributed.

*Read the next few pages about Wills and then read over the Will form in this section.*

*What exactly is a will anyway?*

It is a legal declaration of a person's intention concerning what shall be done following death, as to the disposition of one's property and the administration of the estate.

There are three characteristics of a will that make it different from other forms of property transfer:

1. The will is **revocable** during life--that is, you can change your mind any time and thus change the will.

2. A will is **inoperative** until death--meaning that its provisions don't take effect until that time.

3. It applies to the situation which exists at the time of death--as to your property holdings and beneficiaries *(those who are to receive the proceeds).*

*What happens if I don't make a will?*

The state in which you reside will make one for you. Incidentally, the term *intestate* is used when you die without a valid will.

If you don't have a will, the Probate Court of your area will appoint someone to manage and distribute your assets, and his/her decisions may be quite different from what you would prefer. In addition, your estate will be charged 3 to 5% of the value of the estate for those services.

The key drawback to your will being written by the State is that the law generally makes no allowances for the differing circumstances and needs of the individual members of your family.

There is a Will following this discussion that you can complete until you can meet with an attorney for a more formal will. Be sure to have your signature witnessed by two independent people and their signatures notarized.

Generally, here is what happens if you don't have a will:

1. All property to spouse IF NO CHILDREN;
2. If children, then 1/3 to spouse and 2/3 to children;
3. If spouse is dead, then to children equally;
4. Court will appoint the administrator;
5. A bond will be required;
6. An inventory of the estate will be required;
7. Court will appoint a Guardian;
8. Bond will be required;
9. An annual accounting will be required of the administrator;
10. Children will acquire control of the assets at 18 years of age;

11. Lawyers will get a percentage of the estate for performing this work.

Of course, these may differ from state to state, but these are fairly typical for most of the 50 states.

*What are the advantages of a will?*

Briefly:
1. Determines to whom property will be distributed;
2. Determines who will supervise the process;
3. Minimizes taxes;
4. Waives bonds and inventory;
5. Eliminates or minimizes estate and inheritance taxes.

*What are the requirements of a will?*

Again these will vary from state to state, but generally these are fairly standard requirements in all states:

1. Must be 18 years or older;
2. Must be signed by the person making the will (called the *testator*);
3. In the case of a formal will, the actual signing of the will must be witnessed by at least two persons *(the witnesses do not have to know what is in the Will nor do they have to read it)*;
4. Witnesses must sign in each other's presence;
5. Witnesses must have no interest in the outcome of the will.

*How often should I review my will?*

You should review and change your will when:

1. There is a change in your marital status;
2. Additional children are born;
3. Any of the persons benefiting under the will pass away;
4. You move to a new state;
5. The law changes;
6. You change beneficiaries, executors, or guardians.

*How do I change a will?*

One of two ways:
1. By a *Codicil* (the simple change of a section or portion of the existing will made by an attorney);
2. By creating a new will and revoking the old one.

Remember, you should **never write on your will in an effort to change it.** The Probate courts may invalidate the will or refuse to recognize the changes if you do.

*What information will I need to take to an attorney to draw my Will?*

Here is the information your attorney needs to know when you visit:

1. Your full name and address;
2. Your spouse's and children's names and birth dates;
3. Who will be your Executor (the person responsibile for carrying out your wishes)?
4. Who do you want as an Alternate Executor?
5. Who will be Guardian of your children?
6. Who will be the alternate Guardian?
7. Who will be the Trustee of property left to the children?
8. Who will be the Alternate Trustee?
9. Description of any specific gifts you want to make and to whom they are to be made;
10. The name of any charity you want to receive a portion of your estate and how much.

*What are the most common mistakes in making wills?*

You should leave the drawing of a will to your attorney, but you can help by being alert to the following pitfalls:

1. Don't assume that you are covered by your spouse's will because you hold property jointly. If you both die together, say in an automobile accident, your jointly owned property might go to probate court.

2. Choose appropriate witnesses to your will. If your will is not signed by proper witnessing at the time you sign it, or if it fails to adhere to the strict requirements of state law, your will may be declared invalid. If possible, don't choose witnesses significantly older than you who might die before you.

3. Name alternate beneficiaries for specific gifts in case the primary beneficiary dies before you.

4. Remember that your beneficiary--not your estate--pays taxes on your gift. You won't benefit the recipient of your Rolls-Royce if he has to sell it to pay the taxes on it. You can, however, shift the tax burden in several ways through proper planning.

5. To avoid tax misunderstandings, ask the beneficiary of a gift to sign a dated receipt that describes it.

6. If you want to exclude a spouse or child from your will, you must specifically state that. A spouse or child not mentioned in a will is called a pretermitted heir. Because the law protects them from the oversight of the person writing the will, they have legal recourse unless they are specifically excluded in the will.

*Who should I get for my Executor, Guardian, and Trustee?*

First, let's define these three important people in your will.

The *executor* is the person who will carry out the instructions in the will. For your executor, consider a close family member, an astute friend, a trusted professional, such as your attorney or accountant, or the trust department of your bank or financial institution.

The *guardian* is the person you choose to be responsible for the care of your minor children.

A *trustee* is the person who administers whatever part of your estate you put into a trust. The trustee's main job is to make prudent investments that protect your beneficiaries. This person or institution should be skilled in managing money.

*Where should I keep my will?*

Give the original copy of your will to your attorney or the trust department of your financial institution, keeping only a copy in your home.

Or, keep it with your other valuable papers but not in the safe deposit box at the bank (the box may be sealed at your death, causing difficulties in retrieving the will). A good place in the house to keep valuable papers is the *refrigerator* since it is fire proof and it doesn't hurt the papers to get cold.

*How can I avoid Probate?*

There are many good books written about this subject, and it is beyond the scope of this course to delve deeply into the subject. However, it should be noted that certain assets don't have to go through a will and therefore are not subject to probate administration:

1. Assets held in joint tenancy and assets placed in a trust.

2. The proceeds from life insurance policies go directly to the person or trust you name as your beneficiary.

3. Most U.S. Savings Bonds, which go directly to the person listed on the face of the bond, if you haven't specified otherwise in your will.

4. You can also establish a revocable living trust. Discuss this with your attorney or financial institution.

Another device used to conserve an estate is the *Trust.* A trust is the transfer of property from the owner to a trustee who will manage the holdings and pay income from them as prescribed in the trust agreement. These instruments must be written very carefully in order to escape the various taxes. Therefore, you should see an attorney for preparing a trust.

## Things Which Cannot Be Willed

*There are several things that you own that cannot dispose of by will. Here is a brief discussion of those items.*

**Insurance.** Your insurance policies are usually payable to a named beneficiary. However, the proceeds of those policies are added to your gross estate for tax purposes unless you do not "own" the policies. You generally own an insurance policy when you can change the beneficiary designation. You probably have named your spouse or children as beneficiaries of your policies and will save money on the executor's commissions because the proceeds do not pass by your will.

*Hint:* Wives should "own" your husband's insurance policies. Pay for them out of your own account (of course, your spouse can pay you). When you own the policy, the funds paid by the insurance company will escape the estate taxes.

**Jointly owned property.** Jointly owned property passes outside the will. This most commonly occurs with bank accounts and real estate. A familiar example of joint ownership occurs when a husband and a wife own their home, and the survivor takes title upon the death of the other.

**Pension benefits.** If your pension benefits are continued in some form after your death, you probably have named a beneficiary. Again this is an asset that passes outside your will. Whether or not the pension benefits are taxable depends on many complex factors. Likewise, if you have purchased U.S. Savings Bonds you have named a beneficiary and cannot dispose of them by will.

**Inherited property.** You cannot dispose of property which you expect to inherit but which you did not in fact receive before your death. However, if your benefactor already has died and you are entitled to the property after an event such as the death of a prior life tenant your interest is deemed "vested" and you may dispose of it by will.

**Professional advice.** In each case mentioned here, you should discuss any questions with a professional knowledgable in this area. Our purpose here is to simply make you aware of these potential problems.

# Last Will and Testament

I,_____of the City of _____,

County of _____and State of _____,

being of sound and disposing mind, memory and understanding, do hereby

make, publish and declare this as and for my last Will and Testament, hereby

revoking and annulling any and all Wills by me at any time heretofore made.

*First.* I order and direct all my just debts, funeral expenses as well as the

cost of administration and settlement of my estate to be paid to my Personal

Representative hereafter named, as soon after my decease as conveniently

may be.

*Second.* All of my estate, real, personal and mixed, of whatever kind and

nature and wheresoever situated, remaining after payment of my debts and

funeral expenses, I give, devise and bequeath unto my_____

_____

_____his/her heirs and assigns, absolutely and in fee.

*Third.* I hereby nominate, constitute and appoint _____

_____to be the Personal Representative of this

last Will and Testament and I direct that he/she shall not be obligated to file

any bond, inventory or appraisement or accounting in any public office or

tribunal whatsoever, and further I hereby give and grant unto my said

Personal Representative full power and authority at any time to sell any real

estate which may at the time form part of my estate, for such price, upon

such terms, in such way and manner as may be deemed wise and to make good and sufficient deeds to the purchaser or purchasers thereof without any obligation on the latter to see to or be responsible for the application of the purchase price.

*In Witness Whereof,* I, the said _____have

hereunto set my hand and seal this _____day of _____, 19__

_____

*Signed, Sealed, Published and Declared* by the above named Testator,____
_____as and for his/her last Will and Testament in the presence of us who have at his/her request and in his/her presence and in the presence of each other hereunto subscribed our names as witnesses hereto.

_____          _____
Witness                                                    Witness

_____          _____

_____          _____
Address                                                    Address

State of _____

County of _____

        Personally appeared before me,_____, a
Notary Public in and for the said state and count, the following Affiants, _____
_____and _____
who, being by me first duly sworn, deposed and said that they have witnessed the above Last Will and Testament at the request of the Testator.

_____          _____
Witness (*same as above* )                    Witness (*same as above* )

        Sworn to and subscribed before me this _____day of _____.
19_____.

_____
NOTARY PUBLIC

My Commission Expires:_____

# Donor Cards

Occasionally people wish to donate their body at death for transplant of organs and other body parts or medical school study. Many states have included an organ donor card on the back of their driver's license.

If you do not have a license that includes such a Donor Card and you wish to have one, we have included one on the next page. You should make a copy or cut it out, complete it, sign it, and keep with your driver's license. It is important in case of death away from home.

Make sure that your family understands your feelings and your plans and that they will carry out your wishes.

# UNIVERSAL DONOR CARD

**UNIFORM DONOR CARD**

OF _____
Print or type name of donor

In the hope that I may help others, I hereby make this anatomical gift, if medically acceptable, to take effect upon my death. The words and marks below indicate my desires.

I give:  (a) _____ any needed organs or parts

(b) _____ only the following organs or parts

_____
Specify the organ(s) or part(s)

for the purposes of transplantation, therapy, medical research or education;

(c) _____ my body for anatomical study if needed.

Limitations or special wishes, if any: _____

---

**Signed by the donor and the following two witnesses in the presence of each other:**

_____        _____
Signature of Donor                   Date of Birth of Donor

_____        _____
Date Signed                            City & State

_____        _____
Witness                                  Witness

This is a legal document under the Uniform Anatomical Gift Act or similar laws.

For further information consult your physician or
**National Kidney Foundation**
116 East 27th Street, New York, N.Y. 10016

# If You Anticipate
# DIVORCE

*If you think divorce is unavoidable, it may help to know some facts about divorce itself, decisions you need to make, and steps you need to take.*

Divorce laws vary from state to state, so it is important to check laws in your state to determine the fine details. The reference room of most libraries have copies of the state laws on divorce.

**Community property states** (Arizona, California, Idaho, Louisiana, Nevada, New Mexico, Texas and Washington state). All properties accumulated during your marriage are assumed to belong to both of you. Property owned before marriage usually is assumed to belong to the original owner. The division between spouses is usually fairly even, although if you have children, the person who keeps them may receive more of the property, perhaps 60%.

**Other states.** Separate property states often assume for the most part that properties accumulated during the marriage belong to your husband. Division of property varies in these states.

No one ever thinks divorce could happen to them, but it does. In the United States well over half of all marriages end in divorce. Our purpose here, in keeping with the theme of the book, **Knowledge is Power,** is to make you aware of your options and possibilities in dealing with the event should it occur.

# CHECKLIST

( ) **Keep good financial records.** It is important to keep records if your money has helped purchase investments because of capital gains tax. The inequality of divorce procedures is a second excellent reason for keeping good records--you can prove which part of the properties are yours.

**Warning:** *If you think divorce is likely and your husband suddenly wants to move to another state, check the divorce laws in that state.*

( ) **Try to work out details with spouse.** Divorce is expensive both emotionally and financially. If you've been married for any length of time and have children, both you and your husband probably will have to change your life style.

( ) **Settlement.** Divorces are expensive. Try to work out details before you meet with the attorneys. Decide the following:
  (1) If you have children, who gets custody of them? If you keep the children, how much child support will their father pay? Child support normally continues until a child reaches 18, gets a full time job, or marries. When and how often will your husband have the children? What extras such as special classes, trips, and equipment will he pay for?
  (2) How is the property going to be divided?
  (3) Specifically who gets what?
  (4) If you live in a separate property state (community property states don't award alimony), do you want your share in a lump sum or alimony?

( ) **Alimony.** If you agree to alimony, be sure to include an escalation clause so that your alimony increases along with your former husband's salary.

**Disadvantages of alimony:**

  (1) Your husband may not make the alimony payments in spite of what the court ordered.
  (2) You have to pay tax on alimony because it is income.
  (3) If you remarry, alimony stops in many cases.
  (4) If you work and make a good salary, the alimony can be reduced.

( ) **Things to be aware of.** If you and your husband try to work out a settlement before calling in the attorneys:

  (1) Avoid listing assets to be divided. Simply state that property will be divided evenly or whatever you decide on. If you start listing assets and their value, you're likely to overlook something important.
  (2) Don't get involved at this time with sentimental objects such

**110**

as photographs, family heirlooms, favorite books and paintings. These can bog down the talks indefinitely. Settle everything else before venturing onto this emotional ground.

**NOTE: Property for children.** If you're buying property for an adult child who's married, make it a personal loan with a written Promissory Note instead of an outright gift. If their marriage should break up, the property then will revert to you legally and can be retained or sold by your child.

---

## WHAT YOU SHOULD RECEIVE AS PART OF YOUR SETTLEMENT

---

(1) **Your husband's life insurance policy.** If you're going to be very short of money, he may agree to continue paying the premiums.

(2) **Your home.** Especially if you have children, this provides children with familiar surroundings and a sense of continuity in spite of other changes in their lives. As part of the settlement, your husband may continue home payments or even pay off the mortgage. Don't forget to provide for maintenance and up-keep expenses and property taxes.

(3) **Homeowner's insurance.** If your husband pays off the mortgage, will he pay the homeowner's insurance?

(4) **Health insurance policies.** If you've been carried on your huband's health and disability insurance policies, you may have to get new policies. Will your husband pay for them? Any children should definitely remain on his policy. Under a new law, you may remain on his company policy for up to three years after divorce, *provided* the premiums are paid separately.

(5) **Dependents.** If your husband pays child support, he also will claim the children as dependents. If you plan to work, it would be advantageous for you to claim one child as a dependent so that you can take the child care deductions. This can save you thousands of dollars in a short period of time.

(6) **Attorney's fees.** Who pays the attorney fees?

*"You can get anything in Life YOU want
IF,
You will just help enough other people
get what they want."*

# If You Are WIDOWED

The loss of a loved one is a very emotional and stressful event. All of us have been through that experience. In an effort to make it easier for you at this difficult time, we have prepared the following forms and checklists for you to use in such event.

Read over the next few pages and complete the forms you can NOW. Then, just remember where the checklists are located in this book so that you will have them when you do need them.

Develop your network of friends NOW who will be your support team later. Since there is so much to be done--starting within hours of the passing of a spouse--you shouldn't try to do it yourself. Use your network and family to help you. Don't be afraid to ask family and friends for help.  Believe it or not, they will be flattered. Delegate responsibilities whenever possible and consult with professionals when necessary.

# STEPS TO TAKE

1. **Don't take any major steps if you can avoid them for 1 year after your husband's death.** Your emotional condition is likely to keep you from thinking rationally enough to sell your home or dispose of other valuable holdings. You need a period to mourn and to decide how to carry on your life.

2. **If your husband has a lengthy illness before death, make sure you take all deductions allowed on your income tax.** These vary somewhat from year to year, but your attorney or accountant can tell you what is deductible at the time.

3. **If your husband had debts, he may have taken out insurance to cover them.** Examine insurance papers to determine this.

4. **If your husband died as a result of an accident, do any of his insurance policies pay extra benefits?** Check with the various travel credit card companies to see if their insurance will pay. (*Some card companies carry automatic life insurance.*)

5. **Do any of his health insurance policies include death benefits?** See if you can stay on the group health plan of your spouse's company.

6. **Go over his pensions carefully to make sure you are not overlooking any benefits.** This includes private pensions, government pensions, and company pensions.

7. **Talk with officials at the Social Security office to see if you and/or your children qualify for payments.** Children under 18 and students under 22 probably qualify. So probably do you if you are over 60 or disabled.

8. **If you and your husband have a joint safe deposit box, you may avoid inconvenience by removing everything from it before the bank knows of his death.** If he is ill prior to death, you can empty the box before his demise.

9. **Destroy your husband's credit cards.** Unless you want to continue to use them, they should be destroyed.

10. **If you're working outside the home, maintain your job.** If not, you may want to find a job. This gives you both income and an outside interest.

11. **Make an inventory of family information and keep in a safe place.**

12. **Make sure you have your own bank account in your legal name.** You need to do this anyway NOW. This way you will have some money for any emergency. Don't forget to keep a traveler's check in your pocket book.

13. **Be careful of opportunists that will be calling on you to fix your roof, or your plumbing or other unnecessary activity.** There are many con artists that watch obituaries in the paper for victims with insurance money.

14. **Complete the Transition Plan Checklist on the next few pages.**

15. **Read over the Veteran's Benefits and the Social Security information requirements immediate following the Transition Plan pages in this section.**

16. **Make a copy of the Vital Statistics page in the front of this book and give it to the Funeral Director.**

17. **Stay busy and redirect, reaim your LOVE.**

## SURVIVAL KEY

**Read this and read this well.**

When something happens to your spouse and you either inherit or acquire a large sum of money as a result, you will have many new "friends" and "advisors" that are willing to help you...and this includes FAMILY...once they learn of your new fortune.

Listen to them, but **UNDER NO CIRCUMSTANCES LOAN THEM ANY MONEY** or GUARANTEE a loan for them. Let me repeat that: **DO NOT LOAN ANYONE, INCLUDING FAMILY** any money or PERSONALLY GUARANTEE a loan for them.

Put your new money into a Certificate of Deposit or some other SAFE investment for a minimum of 1 year...preferably some non-speculative investment **that you can't touch** for that time. Resist the temptation to invest in new start-up companies or in any "get rich quick" programs. You will be very vulnerable to these kinds of salespersons, so be careful.

You may have children who need the money, but you will be doing them a great DISSERVICE and yourself a disservice if you give them money or even loan it to them. The first year after you become single will be a very trying time for you both emotionally and psychologically. Don't move fast with any major decisions regarding moving, money or rapid change of life style for at least **1 YEAR** after you become single.

You may need the money you attain for other matters for yourself as time goes on so don't squander it. It may be the last major funding you receive so make it last.

**Remember 1 YEAR!**

# TRANSITION PLAN CHECKLIST

## AT ONCE

1. Make funeral arrangements.  ( )
2. Decide on obituary notice.  ( )
3. Notify relatives.  ( )
4. Notify friends.  ( )
5. Open a new checking account in your name. *(Be sure to have an additional person able to sign checks)* .  ( )
6. Remove contents from safety deposit box.  ( )
7. Remove funds from joint accounts and place in your personal account by writing a check to yourself for the funds and depositing it in your own account.  ( )

## WITHIN THE FIRST 30 DAYS

1. Get 10 certified copies of death certificate.  ( )
2. Put all joint checking and savings accounts in your name.  ( )
3. Establish an "estate" bank account.  ( )
4. Notify all insurance companies and file claims.  ( )
5. Review the auto insurance for accidental death, medical, or other coverages.  ( )
6. Check the medical policies for any time limitations for filing claims and additional coverages.  ( )
7. Check for travel accident coverage.  ( )
8. Report death to Social Security.  ( )
9. Apply for Social Security benefits.  ( )
10. Report death to Veteran's Administration and apply for benefits.  ( )
11. Notify spouse's employers or associates to file for benefits such as retirement and deferred compensation.  ( )
12. Check on Workers Compensation benefits.  ( )

13. Check on spouse's possible life insurance coverage with clubs, associations, credit cards, or other organizations. ( )
14. Have securities transferred to your name. ( )
15. Have U.S. Savings bonds placed in your name. ( )
16. Open a safe deposit box in your "company" name. ( )
17. Notify IRA and Keogh accounts. ( )
18. Check with spouse's employer for health insurance to see if you can continue on the company plan. ( )
19. Other:_____ ( )
20. Other:_____ ( )

## WITHIN THE NEXT 60 DAYS

1. Select an attorney to represent your interest and to file spouse's will. ( )
2. Pick an accountant for financial affairs and for filing estate and inheritance tax returns. ( )
3. Transfer real estate title to your name. ( )
4. Transfer title on cars to your name. ( )
5. Change name on auto and homeowner's insurance policies. ( )
6. Cancel or change all credit or charge cards to your name ( )
7. Change name under which utilities are billed . *(Use your initials, not your name: S.B. Jones not Sue B. Jones.)* ( )
8. Review the beneficiaries on your own life insurance policies ( )
9. Review your own medical insurance policies. ( )
10. Review your will. ( )
11. Notify creditors of your situation. ( )
12. Select a financial advisor. ( )
13. Other:_____ ( )
14. Other:_____ ( )

# Social Security Instructions

**Location of nearest Social Security office is:**

City_____ State_____

## SOCIAL SECURITY BENEFITS

The least known of all social security benefits are those payable at the time of death.

Social Security benefits are **not** paid automatically; application must be made on prescribed forms and specific documents must be furnished.  Further, the law sets a definite time limit on some claims.

To facilitate receiving Social Security benefits you will **need the following** when you contact your Social Security office:

( )  **Marriage certificate**

( )  **Children's birth certificate**

( )  **Proof of widow's age if 62 or older**

( )  **Social Security number**

( )  **Total wages paid on W-2 form or Schedule "C"**

( )  **Death certificate**

( )  **Divorce decree, if applicable**

**NOTES:**

1. Social Security pays a lump sum death benefit. The amount will be determined by past earnings. Maximum death payment is $255.

2. It usually requires about 3 months for a widow to start obtaining Social Security benefits.

3. Your life insurance agent can be most helpful in coordinating Social Security benefits, insurance benefits, and any Veteran's benefits.

4. For any questions about the status of your Social Security Account write: Social Security Administration, P.O. Box 20,Wilkes-Barre, PA 18703, *(use the form found in this book on page 131-132).*

# Veteran's Benefits

Veterans discharged under conditions other than dishonorable are entitled to various benefits, depending upon the status of the serviceman. Application for any or all of these benefits in no way conflicts with claims made under the Social Security Law.

It must be noted, however, that Veterans' benefits will not be paid automatically. Claims for such benefits must usually be made within two years from the date of final interment.

A veteran is generally entitled to a burial payment of about $250 plus other benefits. To facilitate receiving Veteran's Benefits, you will need the following when you contact the Veteran's Administration Office:

( ) **Copy of Death Certificate**

( ) **Proof of Widowhood -- Proof of marriage should be established by one of the following kinds of evidence, in this order of preference:**

>   a. **A properly certified copy of the public or church record of your marriage.**
>
>   b. **Affidavit of clergyman or magistrate who performed the ceremony.**
>
>   c. **Original marriage certificate**
>
>   d. **Affidavits of at least two eye-witnesses to the ceremony**

( ) **Proof of Termination of Marriage -- The termination of all marriages contracted by either of you should be substantiated by certified copies of the final decrees of divorce or annulment, or by proof of death.**

( ) **Proof of Age and Relationship of Child(ren) -- To establish the fact of each child, you should supply a birth certificate or a properly certified copy of the church record of birth or baptism showing the date and the names of the parents.**

# SHORT TIPS FOR ALL WOMEN

*Here are some tips that may help you make decisions on various questions.*

1. Don't put your parents or relatives that are drawing SSI Benefits on your bank signature card. They may lose their benefits.

2. Financial institutions are often simply unable to locate the rightful owners of assets they hold. You can avoid this situation by keeping the appropriate information in this book and informing all your heirs and relatives.

3. If you want to keep your important papers at home, keep them in a fireproof box or in the refrigerator. (It is fireproof.)

4. The easiest way to set up your budget is to look over the cancelled checks for the last year. Itemize each on a sheet of paper by category such as utilities, insurance, etc. Use that sheet as a starting point.

5. Wives should own your husband's life insurance policies. You escape various taxes that way. Let him make a gift of the policies to you and you pay the remainder of the premiums. Talk with your agent about it.

6. If your debt obligation is so cirtical that it requires immediate relief from all debts, big and small, you should consider a little known federal law--the WAGE EARNERS PLAN--which, although it is administered by the bankruptcy courts, has absolutely nothing to do with bankruptcy. You can do it yourself without an attorney for about $25. Check with the local bankruptcy referee for more information.

7. Don't waste money buying credit card protection. You don't need it. You are only obligated for $50 for the fraudulent use of your card in most cases.

8. Try to pay for repairs to your car by credit card. If it isn't repaired to your satisfaction, you simply advise the credit card company that the amount is in dispute, and they won't pay until it is settled to your satisfaction.

9. Have a relative or friend photograph every room in your house/apartment. Keep the prints and the negatives of the rooms in a safety deposit box or some other location away from your house. You may need these pictures to prove ownership later.

10. You need to keep emergency funds available sufficient to pay all of your expenses for 3 to 6 months, depending upon your age and need for security.

# INVESTMENTS

In many instances insurance proceeds and other benefits come into the hands of women when they suddenly become *singlized*. These proceeds can be considerable. What will you do with the check for $10,000, $20,000 or even a $100,000?

It is beyond the scope of this book to go into detail on the investment possibilities but a brief discussion will help guide you.

**A Word of Caution.** There are people out there who watch the papers for the names of widows and divorcees who are apt to come into a sizeable sum of money. These are con artists who will try to convince you to do everything from allowing them to replace your roof to help you invest your new money in speculative risk ventures. Even your relatives will come to you for "loans" to help them. Here is our advice: **DON'T.** Don't make any loans or buy anything that is out of the ordinary for at **least 1 year.** This will give you time to think through any investment possibility.

Some of your investment options include:

- Tax-free money market and mutual funds
- Taxable money market and mutual funds
- Treasury bills
- Certificate of deposit with fixed yield for safety
- Long-term tax-free municipal bonds
- Government money market mutual funds
- Intermediate-term tax-free municipal bonds
- Government money market mutual funds
- Treasury or high grade corporate bond funds
- Ginnie Mae mutual funds
- IRA
- Common or preferred stock
- Real Estate
- Real estate limited partnership
- Gold shares
- Others

*Don't invest in the stock market unless you can afford to lose the amount you invest.*

When you first receive the money, put all but about $5,000 into a Certificate of Deposit for 1 year. That way you will be discouraged from spending any of the money on unnecessary emotional expenses. Put the $5,000 in your savings account at the bank for routine household expenses.

**121**

## "The Life You Lead IS
The Lesson You Teach."

# Before ANYTHING Happens...

While you are in complete control of your emotions, i.e., NOW, complete the forms on the next few pages for future reference.

Send the copy of the Social Security form to the address shown to determine the amount of Social Security you are entitled to receive.

Don't consider any of these forms as morbid, rather think in terms of peace of mind and proper planning. Every successful venture is the result of a plan. This book is your plan for your emotional survival. **Knowledge is Power.**

# FUNERAL/BURIAL PREFERENCES
### Check the following Yes/No spaces as they pertain to your wishes.

**YES    NO**

_____ _____ 1. I direct that my body be used for medical purposes and that my organs be donated as indicated on my Donor Card with my driver's license.

_____ _____ 2. I request post-mortem examination be made if desirable.

_____ _____ 3. I direct cremation of remains.
  (a) Ashes to remain.
  (b) If "a" is Yes, the disposition of the ashes should be as follows:_____
  _____ .

_____ _____ 4. I request burial in the following manner:
  (a) Place of burial: _____
  (b) Address: _____

_____ _____ 5. I wish memorial service with no casket present.

_____ _____ 6. I desire a funeral with remains present.
  (a) Closed casket.
  (b) Open casket.

_____ _____ 7. Service:
  (a) Church:_____
  (b) Minister: _____
  (c) Prelude: _____
  (d) Solo: _____
  (e) Hymns: _____
  (f) Special scripture or poems: _____
  _____

_____ _____ 8. I request that memorial gifts be given to the following organizations: _____
  _____
  _____
  _____

_____ _____ 9. Other information that I desire: _____
  _____

Dated:_____    Signed: _____

**124**

# Memorial Instructions (male)

**In calm recognition of the inevitable, I have given somber thought and you will find the following arrangements are in accordance with my wishes:**

I have arranged _____ I have not arranged but prefer _____

Funeral Home _____

Address _____

City _____ State _____

Phone ____ ( ____ ) ____ - _____

_____ I own property in _____ I do not own property but prefer:

Name of Cemetery _____
Address _____ Phone ( ___ ) ____ - _____
City _____ State _____

Location of Deed _____

Church affiliations: _____
Clergyman desired: _____

Fraternal affiliations: _____

I would like the following to serve as pallbearers:
_____
_____
_____
_____
_____
_____

I request that not over $ _____ be spent on my funeral.

I would prefer the following musical selections:
_____
_____
_____

Special requests:
_____
_____

At my request _____ has consented to carry out these wishes. Phone ( ___ ) ____ - _____ .

## Persons to be notified at the time of my death (husband)

*(Use a pencil)*

**Relatives to be notified:**

Name_____ Phone_____
Address_____Relationship_____
Name_____ Phone_____
Address_____Relationship_____
Name_____ Phone_____
Address_____Relationship_____
Name_____ Phone_____
Address_____Relationship_____
Name_____ Phone_____
Address_____Relationship_____
Name_____ Phone_____
Address_____Relationship_____
Name_____ Phone_____
Address_____Relationship_____
Name_____ Phone_____
Address_____Relationship_____
Name_____ Phone_____
Address_____Relationship_____

**Special friends to be notified:**

Name_____ Phone_____
Name_____ Phone_____
Name_____ Phone_____
Name_____ Phone_____
Name_____ Phone_____
Name_____ Phone_____
Name_____ Phone_____
Name_____ Phone_____
Name_____ Phone_____
Name_____ Phone_____

**Organizations**

Name_____
Address_____ Phone _____

Name_____
Address_____ Phone _____

## Memorial Instructions (female)

In calm recognition of the inevitable, I have given somber thought and you will find the following arrangements are in accordance with my wishes:

I have arranged _____ I have not arranged but prefer _____

Funeral Home _____

Address _____

City _____ State _____

Phone ____( )____ - _____

_____ I own property in _____ I do not own property but prefer:

Name of Cemetery _____
Address _____ Phone ( )____ - _____
City _____ State _____

Location of Deed _____

Church affiliations: _____
Clergyman desired: _____

Fraternal affiliations: _____

I would like the following to serve as pallbearers:

_____
_____
_____
_____
_____
_____

I request that not over $ _____ be spent on my funeral.

I would prefer the following musical selections:

_____
_____
_____

Special requests:

_____
_____

At my request _____ has consented to carry
out these wishes. Phone ( )____ - _____ .

## Persons to be notified at the time of my death (wife)

*(Use a pencil)*

**Relatives to be notified:**

Name_____ Phone_____
Address_____Relationship_____
Name_____ Phone_____
Address_____Relationship_____
Name_____ Phone_____
Address_____Relationship_____
Name_____ Phone_____
Address_____Relationship_____
Name_____ Phone_____
Address_____Relationship_____
Name_____ Phone_____
Address_____Relationship_____
Name_____ Phone_____
Address_____Relationship_____
Name_____ Phone_____
Address_____Relationship_____
Name_____ Phone_____
Address_____Relationship_____
Name_____ Phone_____
Address_____Relationship_____

**Special friends to be notified:**

Name_____ Phone_____
Name_____ Phone_____
Name_____ Phone_____
Name_____ Phone_____
Name_____ Phone_____
Name_____ Phone_____
Name_____ Phone_____
Name_____ Phone_____
Name_____ Phone_____
Name_____ Phone_____

## Organizations

Name_____
Address_____ Phone _____

Name_____
Address_____ Phone _____

# EMERGENCY CASH PLAN

**PRIMARY SOURCES OF READY CASH**

Extra reserve maintained in checking account     $_____

Overdraft limit in checking account     $_____

Savings Account     $_____

Money market funds     $_____

Cashable securities (stocks and bonds)     $_____

Credit card limits     $_____

Prearranged undisbursed loan     $_____

**TOTAL READY CASH FROM PRIMARY SOURCES**     $_____

**SECONDARY SOURCES OF IMMEDIATE CASH**

Borrow on cash value of life insurance     $_____

Borrow from Credit Union     $_____

Borrow from profit-sharing plan     $_____

Borrow from personal loan companies     $_____

Secure loan on car or increase present loan     $_____

Sell second car     $_____

Take out second or third mortgage on home     $_____

Change income tax withholding     $_____

Pawn Jewelry     $_____

Borrow from friends and/or relatives     $_____

Secure loan from employer     $_____

Emergency cash in Keogh or IRA accounts     $_____

**TOTAL POTENTIAL CASH FROM ALL SOURCES**     $_____

129

# SOCIAL SECURITY INFORMATION FOR EVERYONE

You need to know how much money has been saved in your account for you at your retirement.

*How do get that information?*

Simply go by your Social Security office nearest you and get a copy of the form on the next two pages OR, tear it out of the book complete it and mail it in. In about 3 weeks you will receive a computer printout of your account from the government.

When you get your copy, check it out very carefully to be sure it is accurate. Report any mistakes immediately to the Social Security office.

*How often should I check this information?*

I suggest that you should check it about once every 5 years or so if you are working. Keep the copies of the computer printouts with this book when you receive them back from the government so that you can compare them with the previous copy.

If you haven't sent a request in recently, DO IT NOW! There is no cost.

# SOCIAL SECURITY ADMINISTRATION

## Request for Earnings and Benefit Estimate Statement

Social Security is a program that touches the lives of nearly all Americans. Although many people think of it as only a retirement program, it is actually a package of protection that provides for you and your family when you retire, become severely disabled, or die. Social Security is a base you can build on, now and in the future, with savings, other insurance, and investments.

To help you plan for your own financial future, I am pleased to offer you a free statement which shows your Social Security earnings history, tells you how much you have paid in Social Security taxes, estimates your future Social Security benefits, and provides some general information about how the program works.

To receive your statement, please fill out the form on the reverse, and mail it to us. You should receive your statement in 6 weeks or less.

Dorcas R. Hardy

DORCAS R. HARDY
Commissioner of Social Security

SOCIAL SECURITY ADMINISTRATION
WILKES-BARRE DATA OPERATIONS CENTER
P.O. BOX 20
WILKES-BARRE, PA 18703

OFFICIAL BUSINESS
PENALTY FOR PRIVATE USE, $300

First
Class
Postage
Required

SOCIAL SECURITY ADMINISTRATION
WILKES-BARRE DATA OPERATIONS CENTER
P.O. BOX 20
WILKES-BARRE, PA 18703

SOCIAL SECURITY . . . It never stops working!

# SOCIAL SECURITY ADMINISTRATION

## Request for Earnings and Benefit Estimate Statement

To receive a free statement of your earnings covered by Social Security and your estimated future benefits, all you need to do is fill out this form. Please print or type your answers. When you have completed the form, fold it and mail it to us.

1. Name shown on your Social Security card:

First    Middle Initial    Last

2. Your Social Security number as shown on your card:

☐ ☐ ☐ – ☐ ☐ – ☐ ☐ ☐ ☐

3. Your date of birth:

Month    Day    Year

4. Other Social Security numbers you may have used:

☐ ☐ ☐ – ☐ ☐ – ☐ ☐ ☐ ☐

☐ ☐ ☐ – ☐ ☐ – ☐ ☐ ☐ ☐

5. Your Sex: ☐ Male ☐ Female

6. Other names you have used (including a maiden name):

7. Show your actual earnings for last year and your estimated earnings for this year. Include only wages and/or net self-employment income subject to Social Security tax.

A. Last year's actual earnings:

$ ☐ ☐ ☐ , ☐ ☐ ☐ . ☐ 0
Dollars only

B. This year's estimated earnings:

$ ☐ ☐ ☐ , ☐ ☐ ☐ . ☐ 0
Dollars only

8. Show the age at which you plan to retire: _____

Form SSA-7004-PC-OPI (6/88) DESTROY PRIOR EDITIONS

9. Below, show an amount which you think best represents your future average yearly earnings between now and when you plan to retire. The amount should be a yearly average, not your total future lifetime earnings. Only show earnings subject to Social Security tax.

Most people should enter the same amount as this year's estimated earnings (the amount shown in 7B). The reason for this is that we will show your retirement benefit estimate in today's dollars, but adjusted to account for average wage growth in the national economy.

However, if you expect to earn significantly more or less in the future than what you currently earn because of promotions, a job change, part-time work, or an absence from the work force, enter the amount in today's dollars that will most closely reflect your future average yearly earnings. Do not add in cost-of-living, performance, or scheduled pay increases or bonuses.

Your future average yearly earnings:

$ ☐ ☐ ☐ , ☐ ☐ ☐ . ☐ 0
Dollars only

10. Address where you want us to send the statement:

Name

Street Address (Include Apt. No., P.O. Box, or Rural Route)

City    State    Zip Code

I am asking for information about my own Social Security record or the record of a person I am authorized to represent. I understand that if I deliberately request information under false pretenses I may be guilty of a federal crime and could be fined and/or imprisoned. I authorize you to send the statement of my earnings and benefit estimates to me or my representative through a contractor.

▼

Please sign your name (Do not print)

Date    (Area Code)  Daytime Telephone No.

**ABOUT THE PRIVACY ACT**

Social Security is allowed to collect the facts on this form under Section 205 of the Social Security Act. We need them to quickly identify your record and prepare the earnings statement you asked us for. Giving us these facts is voluntary. However, without them we may not be able to give you an earnings and benefit estimate statement. Neither the Social Security Administration nor its contractor will use the information for any other purpose.

☐ SP

# FINAL REVIEW

*(Below are questions that you should ask yourself after finishing this workbook. The page numbers after the questions indicate the page in the workbook where information on the questions can be found.)*

( ) Have you learned the location and how to use the main water shut-off valve, gas valve and the master fuse or electrical circuit breaker in your home or apartment? *p.17.*

( ) Did you look up and record the telephone numbers of the various utilities and their emergency numbers? *p. 19.*

( ) Do you know where your family's important papers and safe deposit keys are located? *p. 23.*

( ) Have you opened a safe deposit box in a "company" name at a bank? *p. 25.*

( ) Did you open your own bank account and begin numbering your checks with 2001? *p. 27.*

( ) Do you know your legal name? Are you sure? *p. 29.*

( ) Did you get a Traveler's check at the bank for $50 and put in your purse for emergencies? *p 31.*

( ) Have you ordered a copy of your Credit Report? *p. 37.*

( ) Did you take steps to establish credit in your own name? *p. 40.*

( ) Do you have a credit card? Do you know the difference between a DEBIT card and a CREDIT card? *pp. 49-51.*

( ) Have you agreed (with yourself) to pay off every credit card each month or else destroy the card? *p. 52.*

( ) Have you gone through the household checks for the last year and prepared your family a budget to live on? *(All successful companies make one!)* *p. 57.*

( ) Do you understand your rights as a consuimer? *p.66.*

( ) How would you buy a new car if your were all alone? *p.68.*

(   ) Do you have life and health insurance?  Did you check with your spouse's employer about continuation of the group health plan if you pay the premiums? *p.78.*

(   ) What about insurance on your possessions and your car?  Do you have enough? Did you list the policies on p. 87? *p.82-86.*

(   ) Have you talked with your spouse or trusted relative about a Power of Attorney should anything happen to you? *p. 91.*

(   ) Have you considered a Living Will for yourself? *p. 97*

(   ) Do you and your spouse have separate Wills?  Where do you keep it?  Do you have an extra copy for review occasionally? *p. 100.*

(   ) Should you suddenly become single, have you agreed not to make any major financial decisions for one year? *p. 115.*

(   ) Did you review the Short Tips on page 120?

(   ) Have you sent your request in for Social Security records? *p. 130.*

(   ) Did you make a list of your important advisors on page 135?

(   ) Have you hand written a legible copy of the WINNERS poem on page 136 and agreed to read it twice each day for 30 days to yourself? Very Important!

(   ) Have you discussed the contents of this book with your spouse and your family and advised them of its location?

(   ) Do you have a friend who can use a book like this? Have you told her about it?

(   ) Have you developed a support system of friends and relatives?

(   ) Are you now aware that the best ways to protect yourself financially against the possibility of widowhood or divorce are:  (1) be able to earn your own living; (2) be aware of financial activities in your marriage (write the family checks to pay bills for a month or so); and (3) if possible, own some property in your own name?

(   ) Do you agree to review this book regularly and update it when conditions

Personal Attorney: _____

Name of Firm: _____

Address: _____

Telephone (Bus.) _____ (Res.) _____

**LIST OF IMPORTANT ADVISORS**

As of

_____

Doctor's Name: _____

Address: _____

Telephone (Bus.) _____ (Res.) _____

Specialty: _____

Personal Accountant: _____

Name of Firm: _____

Address: _____

Telephone (Bus.) _____ (Res.) _____

Personal Banker: _____

Name of Bank: _____

Address: _____

Telephone (Bus.) _____ (Res.) _____

Insurance Agent: _____

Name of Firm: _____

Address: _____

Telephone (Bus.) _____ (Res.) _____

Dentist's Name: _____

Address: _____

Telephone (Bus.) _____ (Res.) _____

# *Final Comments:*

Now you have finished this workbook. Congratulations! Keep the book handy and in a location with your other valuable papers. You will have peace of mind just knowing that you now have the information in one location should anything ever happen.

The last request I want to make of you is for you to copy the poem below in your own handwriting and read it each morning and each evening for one month. You will find that by doing so you will program your subconscious mind, like a computer, to confirm that you are a WINNER!

# WINNER

*If you think you are beaten, you are.*
*If you think you dare not, you don't.*
*If you like to win, but you think you can't,*
*It is almost certain you won't.*

*If you think you'll lose, you're lost,*
*For out of the world we find,*
*Success begins with a woman's will--*
*It's all in a state of mind.*

*If you think you are outclassed, you are.*
*You've got to think high to rise,*
*You've got to be sure of yourself before*
*You can ever win a prize.*

*Life's battles don't always go*
*To the stronger or faster person,*
*But sooner or later the woman who wins*
*Is the woman who thinks she can.*

-Unknown-